BEST AUSTRALIAN
POLITICAL CARTOONS
2024

Russ Radcliffe created the annual *Best Australian Political Cartoons* series in 2003. His other books include: *Man of Steel: a cartoon history of the Howard years* in 2007; *Dirt Files: a decade of Australian political cartoons* in 2013; and *My Brilliant Career: Malcolm Turnbull, a political life in cartoons* in 2016.

Russ has edited collections from some of Australia's finest political cartoonists, including Matt Golding, Judy Horacek, Bill Leak, Alan Moir, Bruce Petty, John Spooner, and David Rowe, and curated several exhibitions including *Moments of Truth*, *Dirt Files*, and *Suppositories of Wisdom*.

In 2013 Russ was awarded the Australian Cartoonists Association's Jim Russell Award for his contribution to Australian cartooning.

For Mark & Ewan

BEST AUSTRALIAN
POLITICAL CARTOONS
2024

edited by
Russ Radcliffe

SCRIBE

Melbourne | London | Minneapolis

Scribe Publications
18–20 Edward St, Brunswick, Victoria 3056, Australia
2 John St, Clerkenwell, London, WC1N 2ES, United Kingdom
3754 Pleasant Ave, Suite 100, Minneapolis, Minnesota 55409, USA

Published by Scribe 2024

Printed and bound in Australia by Ligare Book Printers

Scribe is committed to the sustainable use of natural resources and the use of
paper products made responsibly from those resources.

Scribe acknowledges Australia's First Nations peoples as the traditional owners and
custodians of this country, and we pay our respects to their elders, past and present.

978 1 761381 39 3

Catalogue records for this book are available from the National Library of Australia.

scribepublications.com.au
scribepublications.co.uk
scribepublications.com

cartoonists

Fiona Katauskas, *The Guardian*

Matt Golding, *The Age*

Introduction

It's hard to imagine that 2024 could have topped the previous few years in the horror and excess stakes, but here we are. The world is in a state of extreme flux, and the relative stability of the old global order continues to crumble. Anyone paying the slightest attention probably feels a little like Le Lievre's terrified world hiding from the latest news behind the couch (p. 123). And, like Katauskas' news avoiders (p. vi), I suspect we would probably feel a whole lot better if we avoided politics altogether.

But, as a wiser person once said, just because you're not interested in politics doesn't mean politics isn't interested in you. If you're lucky, you live in the more comfortable parts of Australia where politics, for the most part, is about cost of living, rent, mortgage, health, and financial security, with social justice issues, rights, and freedoms some way down that list. All significant, obviously, but not as consequential as a missile in your kids' playground, a bulldozer knocking down your home, or a bunch of marauding terrorists or ethnic-cleansing militias threatening you — not because of what you've done, but because of who you are.

Of course, it's all relative. And in prosperous Australia, these relativities are starkly apparent in the profound and seemingly intractable disparities in opportunity, education, and health for Indigenous people. The failure of the Voice referendum felt like a kick in the guts for many First Nation's people, and, to many, more shameful proof of the endemic racism and unwillingness to properly recognise the Indigenous people of this country (p. 8). When it comes to renovating the Constitution and truly acknowledging our history, this national conservatism is akin, for Pope, to living with the 'olds' in a 'permanent colonial heritage listing' (p. 12).

It was a negative result in more than one sense for Albanese. He was praised for keeping his promise to hold the referendum, and criticised for his naivete in not postponing it when the Coalition withdrew its support; at the same time, he was blamed for his vapid public support for the Yes case, and condemned for pitching a divisive proposal based on racial grievance. Indeed, the Voice became the first battle in Peter Dutton's full-blown culture-war campaign, casting Albanese as the representative of a divisive elite more concerned with woke cultural matters than the daily realities that most punters were really worried about. Labor's silence on Indigenous affairs and its reluctance to follow through on other aspects of the Uluru statement is testimony to the effectiveness of Dutton's first victory (p. 16).

If the Voice was a crucial energising moment in Dutton's populist rebranding of the Coalition as the party of the working 'man', its trajectory dates back to John Howard's defensive attempts in the late 1990s to incorporate, or at least to not alienate, the Hansonite challenge. Dutton's ascendancy signals the final defeat of Malcolm Turnbull's rearguard attempt to shore up the Coalition as a broad liberal church. Dutton is following the path of right-wing populism and polarisation trodden by Trump, the Brexiteers, Modi, Orban, et al. It is, by now, a familiar story: position yourself as an outsider, a battler against elites; amplify discontent between class, racial, and regional groups; selectively attack unpopular corporate interests; and present simple solutions to complex problems.

His particular brand of populism depends on a pitch to the outer-suburban working-class vote (though not to the trouble-making union type), while apparently abandoning the Liberal urban heartlands lost to the Teals in 2022. It's hard to imagine those increasingly socially progressive heartlands warming to Dutton's crude conservatism any time soon. The old maxim that parties win from the centre is being torn up by Dutton. It's a high-risk strategy designed not to placate or recover its base, but rather to redefine it.

This kind of divisive politics does not arise in a vacuum. It only achieves traction when there are entrenched economic and social problems that deep-rooted assumptions and policy dogmas seem unable to address. The failure of the economy to satisfy the needs of a large chunk of the population is clearly Labor's prime vulnerability. The fact that these problems were inherited from a previous government, after almost a decade in power, doesn't absolve them. The high cost of living, lack of affordable housing, and declining health and education options are obviously the central concerns of most people and the prism through which criticism and attacks on government are refracted.

The relationship between levels of migration with housing and infrastructure is clearly a legitimate conversation, but one wide open to political exploitation, as pointed out, to her cost, by Laura Tingle (p. 26). The door was opened wider by a High Court decision releasing convicted non-citizens and asylum-seekers into the community (p. 22). During the Dunkley by-election held in March 2024, short-term politics outweighed any consideration of the significant threat to social solidarity when Sussan Ley, in a crass Trumpian ploy, raised the spectre of foreign criminals released into the community to assault Aussie women (p. 30). It didn't pay off.

The much-resented Coles/Woolworth duopoly presented an ideal wedge opportunity for Dutton to align himself with ordinary folk struggling under the cost-of-living burden (p. 78). Supported by the Greens, he promised to break up their cosy arrangement — though how exactly was unclear — in what was always going to be a popular pitch. In rejecting the idea, Labor, as a party of the left, ceded what should have been a home-ground advantage, placing it in the invidious position of appearing to defend the heartless cartel behaviour of major corporations.

The attempt to characterise Labor as economically out of touch hit a hurdle over its abandonment of the promised Stage 3 tax cuts (p. 68). Labor had waved them through while in opposition, as a weak-kneed ploy to remove any point of differentiation with Scott Morrison. Albanese's primary electoral pitch was based on doing things differently, and that meant always keeping his word. Delivering the cuts became a totemic guarantee of his integrity, so their abandonment gifted a perfect Coalition gotcha (p. 70). But it turned out that most punters preferred the redistribution of the high-end cuts into their wallets to keeping an imprudent promise to the relatively well-off.

With 'A Future Made in Australia', Labor made much of its ambition for Australia to become a renewable-energy superpower supporting an economy based on clean and smart manufacturing (p. 88). The reignition of the climate wars was predictable, given the Abbottoid Dutton (p. 54) and the significant Greens presence in parliament. For the Greens, Labor's road to net zero continues to depend on massive new fossil-fuel projects, locking us into the future hell of anthropogenic catastrophe — proof to them that Labor's climate hypocrisy was little better than the Coalition neo-denialism (p. 50).

Dutton's threat to withdraw from the 2015 Paris Climate Agreements and to embrace nuclear energy was the centrepiece of the Coalition's attack on Labor's energy policy (p. 56). With its hallucinatory promise of boundless cheap, clean, baseload energy, it was the solution to expensive domestic power prices. Why hadn't someone thought of such a bold and adventurous solution before. Labor, signed up to its own impetuous nuclear extravagance — AUKUS — could hardly repeat previous generations' principled rejection of nukes. But the proposal lacked any supporting technical or economic argument, and the avalanche of expert opinion on why it was untenable suggested that generating political distraction rather than electricity was the point (p. 60).

The nuclear option also signalled another ideological rebranding, with the party of free enterprise proposing massive government investment in an industry that private capital wouldn't go near. With the added benefit of undermining the continuing investment in actual renewables, and the necessity of reliance on fossil fuels for decades to come, it invited, cui bono, the question of which interests were truly served by Dutton's 'rollout of delayables' (p. 64).

•

While the US, Israel, and other major players in the region were congratulating themselves on the most stable Middle East in decades, and contemplating the potential of the Abraham accords, Hamas was planning to remind the world that they would not be dealt out of this cosy arrangement and that the Palestinian cause could not be sidelined.

Israel lives under a constant threat from, among others, Iran and its proxies. Nuclear-armed and with the most powerful military in the region, Israel is backed up by the most powerful military force in the world. But the threat of small-scale attacks and miscalculations escalating to a major conflict is never far away. American aircraft carriers in the Gulf provide no protection against hang-gliding commandos.

Hamas's attack on southern Israel on 7 October 2023 was shocking in its rapidity, scale, and sheer brutality (p. 122). With over 1,000 deaths and 251 hostages abducted, it was the most traumatic event in Israel since the Yom Kippur War. It was also an indictment of the complacency and basic security failures of the Netanyahu government. History did not start with this event. It is an episode in a long and continuing story of the Israeli occupation and humiliation of Palestinians in Gaza and the West Bank — a history pervaded by cruelty, bad faith, and intransigent and unrealisable demands on all sides.

Israel's immediate desire for revenge was understandable, if ill considered. Its response, by any measure, has been brutal, with tens of thousands of civilian deaths, and the cities and towns of Gaza laid to waste (p. 128). A state's first duty is, of course, to defend its people, but to question where self-defence ends and collective punishment or revenge begins is entirely legitimate.

The 'effrontery' of the International Criminal Court's application for an arrest warrant for Benjamin Netanyahu — the first for a Western leader — sparked outrage and accusations of antisemitism (p. 136). Why, among all the horrors committed in the contemporary world, single out Israel? The alternative question is, of course, why should any state be given a free pass? (p. 134).

The ICC is an expression of moral purpose by the West — part of a redemptive project born out of the catastrophic wars of the twentieth century, with the Shoah as its pivotal moral reference. Despite the ICC's high-minded purpose, things look quite different when viewed from the global south: the exemption of Western nations from its jurisdiction feeds a perception of the rules-based international order as being selective and hypocritical, and primarily an instrument of victors' justice. Hence, the case brought by South Africa against this most compelling national expression of the West's redemption carries extraordinary symbolic power.

From Bill Clinton to Joe Biden, Netanyahu has long been expert at manipulating US domestic politics. A generation unambiguously supportive of an idealised vision of a liberal, democratic Israel, exemplified by Biden, is passing. And Israel has changed under his leadership. As extensive demonstrations around the world attest, younger generations are likely to see Israel not as a small, threatened nation, but as an aggressor: highly militarised, internally democratic, yet subjugating a large adjacent population, and governed by a crooked leader who depends on extreme ethno-nationalists for his survival. It's a view shared by many oppositional groups within Israel, though often charged with being antisemitic by many Western supporters (p. 136).

In Australia, home to one of the largest post-Holocaust Jewish diasporas in the world, and to a large migrant population from around the Middle East, the cultural stresses and sensitivities are particularly intense (p. 140). The reduction of both Jewish and pro-Palestinian opinions to caricatures and singular voices and interests is one of the more disturbing sleights of hand being perpetrated as the war in Gaza is incorporated into a domestic culture war. Accusations of antisemitism — the paradigmatic racial prejudice — and Islamophobia are regularly tossed around. This often-cynical instrumentalisation for short-term political benefit undermines the seriousness and reality of both tendencies.

When does legitimate anger at or criticism of the behaviour of a state flip into racist tropes; and when does support for a brutalised people become an apologia for terror? These aren't academic questions. The ability of diverse communities to live together in the future depends on the way they are asked and answered now.

For all the party's historical empathy and support for the justice of the Palestinian cause, Labor's inflexibility over Fatima Payman's crossing of the floor demonstrated a tin-eared failure to recognise the depth of feeling — across all communities — about the plight of Gaza. Her exile in the same week that Labor appointed a hawkish Israel supporter as an antisemitism envoy reinforced a perception that, for it, human rights, pain, and suffering are weighted differently (p. 147).

If Labor's political tightrope walk between pro-Likud and pro-Palestinian Australians was often clumsy and contradictory, Dutton's demand that, on principle, Palestinian refugees be refused entry visas marked a new and cynical low, even for him (p. 148). His record of incendiary racial provocations and dog-whistles were some of the most egregious and socially damaging by a senior politician in recent memory. It remains as true here in Australia as it is in the Middle East that there can be no security or peace, let alone flourishing, until everyone feels secure.

The global implications of the Gaza conflict are profound, and Labor's response was clearly influenced by our foreign policy. It seemed inconceivable that Labor would adopt any stance towards Israel/Palestine that was out of a close lockstep with US policy. Whatever room to manoeuvre or nimbleness we could have displayed in global affairs has been jeopardised by that tightening strategic embrace and the chimera of AUKUS (p. 160).

The conflict also peels away another layer of the veil of US power. Despite providing its ultimate defensive shield, the US's ability to influence Israel has been minimal; on Gaza, its impotence has been embarrassing (p. 138). Whatever remained of the US's moral standing in the eyes of the global south after Iraq, it was in free fall after Gaza. It was no coincidence that US-led sanctions on Russia for its Ukraine invasion were largely applied only by its Western allies. Even Quad partner India welcomed a visit from Vladimir Putin with a hug.

It was hard to take our eyes off the unreality show that was US politics in 2024 — one of the most extraordinary years in US history (p. 162). The wholly owned Trump subsidiary — the Republican Party — maintained the rage about the stolen 2020 election. The Democrats prayed at the altar of the court system for salvation from a second Trump presidency. Neither side was able to agree on any particular set of facts, other than that the other side posed an existential threat to US democracy. Bewitched by this show, neither the Democrats nor the American media acknowledged the declining capacity of the president — something that poll after poll indicated was a serious electoral problem. It took Biden's disastrous showing in the first presidential debate in late June to provoke a response (p. 170).

The failed assassination attempt on Trump was obviously lifted from the rejected script of a very clichéd movie (p. 172). The ultimate showman, even in his most vulnerable moment, Trump had an almost preternatural sense of the camera and the historical moment. And extraordinarily good luck. The iconography of that photograph seemed suspiciously perfect — even staged or rehearsed. Was it a piece of Trump media management? Or the deep state's ill-fated revenge? The very immediacy of the responses took away from the gravity of what had just happened. A nation-defining moment of truth descended into the idiot kitsch of mythmaking and conspiracy, even before the Secret Service got him into the car.

How politically motivated the shooting was is still an open question. 'Assassination' seems like too big a word for the actions of an angry, alienated kid enabled by crazy gun laws — more like one of the school shootings that are such a depressingly regular feature of American life.

Either way, the messianic narrative had cosmic validation: they mocked, cheated, persecuted, and tried to kill him, but he was surely saved for a higher purpose. The election was a lock! Until Biden did the right thing, eventually, and made way for Kamala (p. 176). And, in a moment, the world switched again.

Labor's goal in its presumed first term of government was to cement its place as the dominant party of the centre, and therefore as the natural party of government for years to come. They tried to set a tone of calm, quiet efficiency with realistic expectations while getting on with the job of repair after a decade of Coalition policy indolence. And efficient government is no small thing. Examples of chaotic and incompetent populist governments both here and overseas are easy to find.

Of course, many on the left view this centrist and incrementalist incarnation of Labor as lacking the radical, reformist imagination of its past — worthy, maybe, but essentially a party of the status quo. Domestically, the failure to substantially improve the economic conditions of the most needy — JobSeeker remains among the lowest unemployment benefits in the developed world — and a perception that Labor's energy policy is fatally compromised, are prime complaints. Internationally, despite the oft-repeated platitudes about our love of regional cooperation, we have now clearly picked a side. As the Australian military becomes ever more deeply absorbed into the command structures of the US, our foreign policy is increasingly directed towards maintaining the illusion of US primacy in the Pacific. That this posture of Chinese containment is of long-term benefit to Australia's national interest is rarely examined beyond the repetition of American national security talking points.

Right-wing populism may have receded in the UK, but it was going strong in Europe and the US, and Dutton was hoping that its tide had not peaked in Australia. Energised by the crushing of the Voice, he was highly effective in carrying a lacklustre Coalition into a competitive position after only one term in opposition. By definition, populists need to be popular. The electoral appeal of identifying and demonising enemies and offering simplistic solutions needs the wit of a Boris Johnson or the media presence of a Donald Trump to carry it off. Peter Dutton is blessed with neither quality. And, with its urban heartlands unlikely to come back anytime soon, the Coalition's road back to government was steep.

Whether Dutton's attempts to redefine Albanese as a representative of the culturally woke rather than working people would convince enough voters will be tested in 2025. Economic circumstances have clearly worked against the government. That Australia is facing the same types of economic pressures as other similar economies cuts little ice electorally. And, with a fundamental realignment of the politics of left and right underway, and the general distrust of the two-party system, the possibility of a future hung parliament is very real.

SISYPHUS HALFWAY INTO HIS FIRST TERM

Matt Golding, *The Age*

'I am someone who believes that we need to restore faith in politics. And one of the ways that we do that is by saying what we will do, and then doing what we have said we would do. That is what we have done tonight. And I make no apologies for that.'

— Anthony Albanese

'We find the polls across the country right now quite consistent. Labor is in the low 30s; the Coalition is in the mid-to-high 30s in terms of primary vote. Not much has really changed since the last federal election. The big change obviously is the honeymoon that Labor was enjoying is now completely gone and dead.'

— Kos Samaras

'If anything, I'm surprised the honeymoon lasted as long as it did.'

— Labor MP, anon

Jon Kudelka, *The Saturday Paper*

Dean Alston, *The West Australian*

Australia says No

David Rowe, *Australian Financial Review*

'I do leave this place with some sense of sorrow, in that as a nation we were not able to respond positively to the referendum. I think that would have helped our country.'
— Pat Dodson

'Yet, despite what must have been such a traumatic experience as a child, he grew into the Father of Reconciliation — a figure of grace, dignity and inspiration. He leaves parliament with our thanks, and with our love.'
— Anthony Albanese

First Dog on the Moon, *The Guardian*

WELCOME MAT to COUNTRY

Christopher Downes, *The Mercury*

'Aboriginal and Torres Strait Islander peoples are in shock and are grieving the result … That people who came to our country in only the last 235 years would reject the recognition of this continent's First Peoples … is so appalling and mean-spirited as to be utterly unbelievable.'
— Open Letter, The Uluru Statement

'We argued for this change not out of convenience but from conviction, because that's what people deserve from their government. And of course, when you do the hard things, when you aim high, sometimes you fall short. And tonight we acknowledge, understand, and respect that we have.'
— Anthony Albanese

'This is the referendum that Australia did not need to have. The proposal and the process should have been designed to unite Australians, not to divide us. What we've seen tonight is Australians literally in their millions reject the prime minister's divisive referendum.'
— Peter Dutton

'Wrecking is always easier than building and looking for someone to blame is much simpler than finding a solution.'
— Anthony Albanese

Cathy Wilcox, *The Sydney Morning Herald*

Peter Broelman, *The Echidna*

David Pope, *The Canberra Times*

'It is clear no reform of the Constitution that includes our peoples will ever succeed.'
— Open Letter, The Uluru Statement

'What I ask for people to think about is that people who aspire to lead this nation in the Coalition, and their behaviour, misinforming people about what the referendum was about and what it could and couldn't do, I think that is the true shame. That is a wasted opportunity.'
— Thomas Mayo

'The past 12 months have shown me that the vast majority of Australians want improvements for those Indigenous Australians who are struggling and that they want change. Australians want governments to do the job that needs to be done to get real, practical outcomes.'
— Nyunggai Warren Mundine

'Success is not final, failure is not fatal: it is the courage to continue that counts.'
— Anthony Albanese, quoting Winston Churchill

Phil Somerville, *somervillecartoons.com*

John Farmer, *The Mercury*

AUSTRALIAN PATENTED COLOUR BLINDNESS TEST

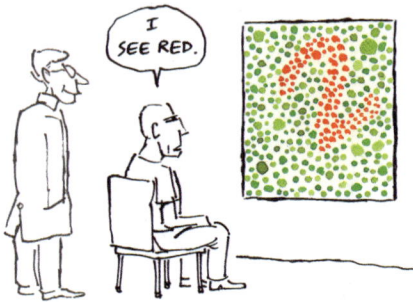

Phil Somerville, *somervillecartoons.com*

Cathy Wilcox, *The Sydney Morning Herald*

'The truth is that the majority of Australians have committed a shameful act whether knowingly or not, and there is nothing positive to be interpreted from it.'
— Open Letter, Uluru Statement

'The Australian people have overwhelmingly voted saying No to the referendum. They have said No to division within our Constitution along the lines of race … They have said No to grievance and the push from activists to suggest that we are a racist country when we are absolutely not a racist country.'
— Jacinta Nampijinpa Price

'This is one of the biggest paradoxes of this referendum … almost nine in ten Australians think it is important for First Nations peoples to have a voice or say in matters that affect them. This includes around three-quarters of No voters.'
— Prof. Nicholas Biddle, Australian National University survey

Matt Golding, *The Age*

'An Albanese Labor Government will establish a Makarrata Commission as a priority … [which] will have responsibilities for overseeing processes for Treaty-Making and Truth-Telling.'
— Anthony Albanese

'It's condescending to everyone who believed in this government's promises, which they are now clearly breaking.'
— Lidia Thorpe

'Well, that's not what we have proposed … What we've proposed is Makarrata just being the idea of coming together.'
— Anthony Albanese

'Under a government I lead there will be no Makarrata and there will be no revisiting of Truth-Telling.'
— Peter Dutton

Jon Kudelka, *The Saturday Paper*

David Pope, *The Canberra Times*

ONLY 9 MORE TROLLING DAYS 'TIL AUSTRALIA DAY

Glen Le Lievre, *Patreon*

'Woolies Goes Woke: supermarket giant cancels Australia Day.'
— *The Daily Telegraph* headline

'There has been a gradual decline in demand for Australia Day merchandise from our stores over recent years. At the same time there's been broader discussion about 26 January and what it means to different parts of the community.'
— Woolworths

'If they don't want to celebrate Australia Day that's a decision for them, but I think people should boycott Woolworths.'
— Peter Dutton

'I think we should be boycotting those who are prepared to not be proud of this country.'
— Jacinta Nampijinpa Price

John Farmer, *The Mercury*

Peter Broelman, *The Echidna*

the political highground

David Rowe, *Australian Financial Review*

'The high court will make its decisions independent of government. No government, no parliament, no minister is above the law. Community safety is the first and foremost responsibility of government.'
— Andrew Giles

'We know what's going to happen, Labor's going to stuff it up, it will end up in the High Court. The Coalition will say the government's incompetent, and there'll be some truth to it, and then we'll have this whole sham process again.'
— David Shoebridge

Glen Le Lievre, *Australian Financial Review*

Andrew Dyson, *The Age*

David Pope, *The Canberra Times*

'Unfortunately, examples of non-cooperation with the government's removal efforts have been going on for too long against the expectations of the Australian community, and undermining the integrity of our migration laws.'
    — Andrew Giles

'Today our government will introduce tough new laws … that will give the Commonwealth power to put in place very strict visa conditions … to ensure the community is kept safe … These include the ability for the Commonwealth to impose ankle monitoring bracelets on people who have been released from detention.'
    — Clare O'Neil

'The way they reacted to the High Court decision shows that the major parties are always united against refugees. It's shown that it's important for these parties to have this competition of cruelty.'
    — Behrouz Boochani

'What a sham this whole process is. It's an ultra-marathon in incompetence.'
    — Dan Tehan

Andrew Dyson, *The Age*

Andrew Dyson, *The Age*

Cathy Wilcox, *The Sydney Morning Herald*

'We have seen some of the most horrific, violent and sexual offenders released into our community, allowed to stay despite being non-citizens, because the AAT has cited Direction 99.'
— James Paterson

'The new revised direction will make crystal clear that the Australian government expects community protection to be given greater weight when it comes to visa decisions.'
— Andrew Giles

'It's just not right that people with no connection to New Zealand are deported to New Zealand.'
— Christopher Luxon

'I want to hear from the minister: how is he going to explain what happens when the first woman who is sent back to Iran under this legislation gets put in prison?'
— Adam Bandt

Jon Kudelka, *The Saturday Paper*

Alan Moir, *www.moir.com.au*

Matt Golding, *The Age*

'It's not just housing. People know that if you move suburbs, it's hard to get your kids into school, or into childcare. It's hard to get into a GP because the doctors have closed their books. It's hard to get elective surgery. These factors have all contributed to capacity constraints because of the lack of planning in the migration program.'
— Peter Dutton

'I have observed on several occasions that there were considerable dangers for the way our political discourse would unfold — and for social harmony — in linking migration to the housing crisis. As the alternative prime minister, with an election approaching within a year, Mr Dutton's comments deserve rigorous scrutiny and examination.'
— Laura Tingle

'I thought Dutton would run off to the right, and I thought he would do a lot of damage as prime minister of Australia in a short period.'
— Malcolm Turnbull

Harry Bruce, *Cairns Post*

Fiona Katauskas, *The Guardian*

Jon Kudelka, *The Saturday Paper*

Fiona Katauskas, *The Guardian*

Cathy Wilcox, *The Sydney Morning Herald*

'I wasn't saying every Australian is a racist … but we clearly have an issue with racism. For some months now, for example, *The Australian* newspaper has been devoting considerable space to its alarm about a rise in antisemitism.'
— Laura Tingle

'Laura Tingle has demonstrated over and again her bias and I think Kim Williams needs to explain why having someone so blatantly partisan sitting in the top political commentator position is in fact acceptable.'
— Jacinta Nampijinpa Price

'The role of senior political correspondents is not to give anodyne summaries of "he said, she said", but rather go into some assessment of analysis of what's been said and what it might mean.'
— Kim Williams

'The question has to be asked, why do we fund something that only wants to talk to half of Australia?'
— Barnaby Joyce

David Rowe, *Australian Financial Review*

'Thug.'
   — Malcolm Turnbull

'If you do not want to see Australian women being assaulted by foreign criminals, vote against Labor.'
   — Sussan Ley

'I don't know, really, you must wake up in the morning, look in the mirror and think, after 25 years of being a member of parliament, is this what I've become ... reduced to putting out tweets like this?'
   — Jason Clare

'You just have a fear campaign about everything and a solution for nothing.'
   — Anthony Albanese

Jon Kudelka, *The Saturday Paper*

Harry Bruce, *Townsville Bulletin*

Peter Broelman, *The Echidna*

'I'm on a prescription drug and they say certain things may happen to you if you drink.'
— Barnaby Joyce

'So what kind of leaders do our communities expect us to be? Do they want serious, responsible people who respect the importance of the laws before us, or do they want larrikin, living, breathing caricatures of Sir Les Patterson?'
— Tania Lawrence

'I leave this place appreciative and thankful, unburdened by offences, and released from any bitterness that can so often haunt post-political lives. This is due to my faith in Jesus Christ, which gives me the faith to both forgive but also to be honest about my own failings and shortcomings.'
— Scott Morrison

'I've seen Scott say so many things that are utterly untrue — he can look you dead in the eye and say something completely opposite to what he's really thinking,'
— Malcolm Turnbull

Mark Knight, *Herald Sun*

Matt Golding, *The Age*

the cost of living

Andrew Dyson, *The Age*

'I pray with all my heart that Cop28 will be another critical turning point towards genuine transformational action at a time when, already, as scientists have been warning for so long, we are seeing alarming tipping points being reached … Despite all the attention, there is 30 per cent more carbon dioxide in the atmosphere now than there was back then, and almost 40 per cent more methane … Some important progress has been made, but it worries me greatly that we remain so dreadfully far off track as the global stocktake report demonstrates so graphically.'
— King Charles

Harry Bruce, *Townsville Bulletin*

John Farmer, *The Mercury*

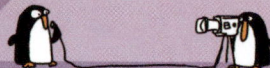

**First Dog
on the Moon,**
The Guardian

Matt Golding, *The Age*

Jon Kudelka, *The Saturday Paper*

Megan Herbert, *The Age*

'The science is clear: the 1.5°C limit is only possible if we ultimately stop burning all fossil fuels. Not reduce, not abate. Phase out, with a clear timeframe.'
— António Guterres

'I accepted to come to this meeting to have a sober and mature conversation. I'm not in any way signing up to any discussion that is alarmist. There is no science out there, or no scenario out there, that says that the phase out of fossil fuel is what's going to achieve 1.5°C.'
— Sultan Al Jaber, president Cop28

'It is incredibly concerning and surprising to hear the Cop28 president defend the use of fossil fuels. It is undeniable that to limit global warming to 1.5°C we must all rapidly reduce carbon emissions and phase out the use of fossil fuels by 2035 at the latest. The alternative is an unmanageable future for humanity.'
— Prof. Sir David King, Climate Crisis Advisory Group

JUST IN THE LAST 50 YEARS I HAVEN'T BEEN FEELING WELL.

I'M THINNING AT MY POLES.

MY OCEAN PRESSURE'S AROUND 200 OVER 90.

MY LUNGS ARE NOT AS GREEN AS THEY USED TO BE.

I'VE GOT CARBON IN MY BLOOD.

I'VE GOT PLASTIC IN MY URINE.

I HAD A RAFT OF TESTS AND SCANS.

TURNS OUT I'VE GOT PARASITES.

ABOUT 8 BILLION.

Somerville

Phil Somerville, *somervillecartoons.com*

39

Glen Le Lievre, *Australian Financial Review*

'All nations of the world have acknowledged … that our future is in clean energy, and the age of fossil fuels will end.'
— Chris Bowen

'The road to net zero runs through WA's resources.'
— Madeleine King

'There's high urgency to making life multi-planetary … Less than five years for uncrewed, less than ten to land people, maybe a city in 20 years, but for sure in 30, civilisation secured.'
— Elon Musk, Mars plan

'Labor promised to fix Australia's broken environment laws, but without stopping native forest logging and fossil fuel expansions, the government will be failing to protect our planet … and its promise to the Australian people.'
— Sarah Hanson-Young

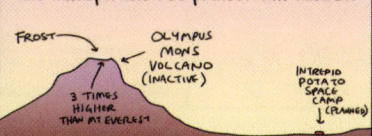

First Dog on the Moon, *The Guardian*

Matt Bissett-Johnson, *Melbourne Observer*

Fiona Katauskas, *The Guardian*

First Dog
on the Moon,
The Guardian

David Pope, *The Canberra Times*

'Our Nature Positive Plan is a win-win: a win for the environment and a win for business.'
— Tanya Plibersek

'Any reforms would have a disproportionate impact here because of the nature of our economy, and the WA resources sector has made it clear that they want more detail and comprehensive consultation on these reforms.'
— Roger Cook, Western Australia premier

'Western Australia doesn't mark my homework.'
— Tanya Plibersek

'There is absolutely no need, on our over-cleared continent, to damage nature to build renewable energy projects.'
— Kelly O'Shanassy, Australian Conservation Foundation

'How can we expect EPA to halt extinctions when the laws that it is enforcing are fundamentally broken?'
— Kate Milla, Birdlife Australia

Jon Kudelka, *The Saturday Paper*

Andrew Weldon, *The Big Issue*

the transition

David Pope, *The Canberra Times*

'Under all credible net zero scenarios, natural gas is needed through to 2050 and beyond … Gas will be essential to the transition because our energy system needs gas to achieve net zero.'
— Madeleine King

'Investment in new gas supply is needed if we are to reach net zero with thriving industries.'
— Ian Davies, Senex CEO

'While Australia is distracted talking about the LNP nuclear charade, the federal government is approving new fossil fuel projects.'
— Rod Campbell, Australia Institute

Fiona Katauskas, *The Guardian*

John Spooner, *The Australian*

THE DISASTER

THE DISASTER READY FUND

FOSSIL FUEL SUBSIDIES

MEGAN HERBERT

Megan Herbert, *The Age*

'Today's announcement is more *Back to the Future* than Future Made in Australia. Australia is already using less gas, so the suggestion we need more of it sounds like Scott Morrison's "gas-led recovery", not Anthony Albanese's "renewable energy superpower".'
— Jennifer Rayner, Climate Council

'The Strategy needs to be backed by clear, tangible actions that urgently unlock new gas supply to address looming shortfalls and provide an unequivocal signal to the market that Australia is committed to ensuring sustainable gas supply to the Australian economy and the region.'
— Samantha McCulloch, Australian Energy Producers

'It is fair to say it costs the Australian public more than it raises once subsidies, tax breaks, and other liabilities — financial and climate-related — are factored in.'
— Australia Institute

Geoff Pryor, *Pearls & Irritations*

Geoff Pryor, *Pearls & Irritations*

Matt Golding, *The Age*

'There is now next to no difference between Labor and the Liberals when it comes to coal and gas.'
— Adam Bandt

'In my opinion, not a cent of public money should be spent on new gas or resources projects that don't help transition us to a low-emissions economy.'
— Josh Burns

'[The plan] struck the right balance by ensuring Australia can transition to net zero, while also keeping prices down, delivering reliable power supply and retaining jobs.'
— Bran Black, Business Council of Australia

'The road to net zero runs through Australia's resources sector.'
— Madeleine King

Jon Kudelka, *The Saturday Paper*

Cathy Wilcox, *The Sydney Morning Herald*

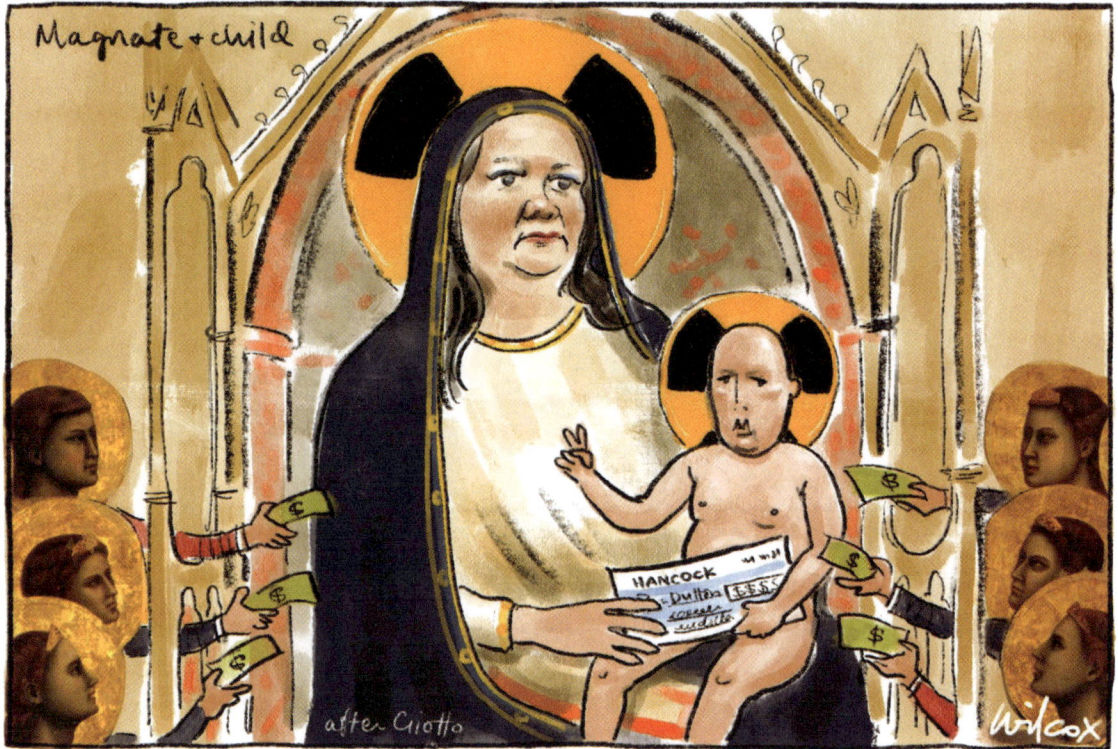

Cathy Wilcox, *The Sydney Morning Herald*

'We are deeply concerned the Nature Positive Plan … will lead to greater uncertainty for business, heightened risk of third-party intervention, approval delays and, fundamentally, material land and resource sterilisation.'
  — mining lobby group letter to PM

'The concern is that this is how politics works in Australia.'
  — Greenpeace

'I paint the world as I see it … People don't have to like my paintings, but I hope they take the time to look and think, why has this Aboriginal bloke painted these powerful people? What is he trying to say?'
  — Vincent Namatjira

'While Rinehart has the right to express her opinions about the work, she does not have the authority to pressure the gallery into withdrawing the painting simply because she dislikes it.'
  — Penelope Benton, NAVA executive director

PASS THE PARCEL

COALITION
NIMBY CENTRAL

Alan Moir, *www.moir.com.au*

HER OBSCENE WEALTH REALLY DOES SEEM TO FOLLOW YOU AROUND THE ROOM.

Jon Kudelka, *The Saturday Paper*

Geoff Pryor, *Pearls & Irritations*

'If the first episode of Australian climate wars was a tragedy, the second is an expensive and dangerous farce.'
— Malcolm Turnbull

Matt Golding, *The Age*

Fiona Katauskas, *The Guardian*

Mark Knight, *Herald Sun*

'I will not sign up to an arrangement where unachievable emissions targets and a reckless 'renewables only' rollout destroys our economy, makes businesses go broke, and sends families bankrupt.'
— Peter Dutton

'Reneging on our national commitment … will damage Australia's diplomatic, economic, and moral standing. We have international investors lined up to back Australia's smart energy revolution … This will send them elsewhere.'
— Richie Merzian, Smart Energy Council

'It's OK for Mr Albanese to want to feel popular and get all the back slaps from Justin Trudeau and Emmanuel Macron at the Paris conferences … The prime minister's responsibility is actually to the Australian public.'
— Peter Dutton

'This might be the dumbest policy ever put forward by a major party. It is the worst combination of economic and ideological stupidity.'
— Jim Chalmers

Cathy Wilcox, *The Sydney Morning Herald*

David Pope, *The Canberra Times*

Jon Kudelka, *The Saturday Paper*

'I think any Australian who thinks climate change is real would think now that Peter Dutton is a real risk … even Tony Abbott didn't pull out of a global agreement on climate change and he thinks it's crap.'
— Jason Clare

'We'd like to look for whatever option we can so we don't have to pursue large-scale renewables full stop.'
— David Littleproud

'My objection to nuclear has never been moral. It is for some people … not for me. It's not a moral or philosophical objection. It is a practical, evidence-based rejection for Australia. It is not the right answer for Australia.'
— Chris Bowen

'There has been a sea-change on this issue … And Labor's response has been pathetic. Fancy having cartoons and memes on a serious subject. Where is the serious intellectual response?'
— John Howard

John Shakespeare, *The Sydney Morning Herald*

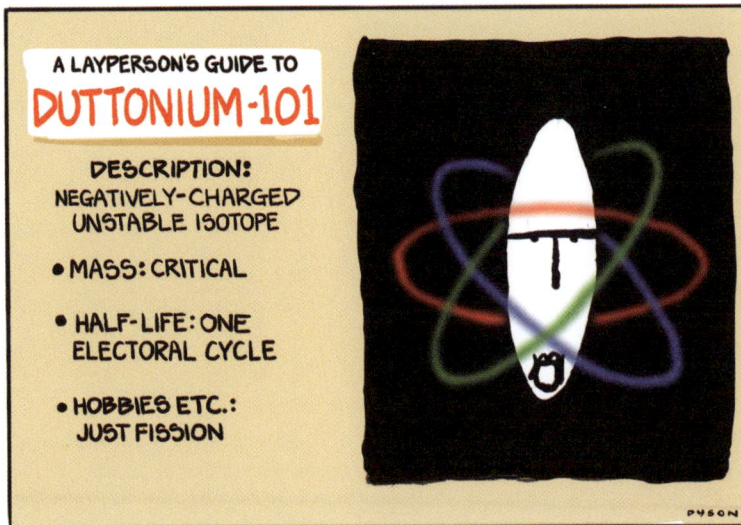

Andrew Dyson, *The Age*

Alan Moir, *The Sydney Morning Herald*

'There is no viable schedule for the regulation or development of nuclear energy in Australia, and the cost, build time, and public opinion are all prohibitive.'
— Damien Nicks, AGL

'The GenCost report is updated each year and provides the very best estimates for the cost of future new-build electricity generation in Australia.'
— Dr Doug Hilton, CSIRO

'It's not a genuine piece of work.'
— Peter Dutton on CSIRO nuclear report

'When you stop debating the scientific merits of ideas, you are … dog-whistling that the science itself is untrustworthy, the scientists are untrustworthy, and there is some grander conspiracy that organisations like CSIRO are part of.'
— Dr Doug Hilton, CSIRO

'At best, Peter Dutton's nuclear proposal would deliver 3.7 per cent of the energy required.'
— John Grimes, Smart Energy Council

Fiona Katauskas, *The Guardian*

Mark David, *independentaustralia.net*

Glen Le Lievre, *Patreon*

'Our prime minister is a man with his mind still captured in his university years, he's as a child in a man's body ... more interested in appeasing the international climate lobby than sticking up for the interests of everyday Australians.'
  — Peter Dutton

'Today Peter Dutton could've answered the many questions Australians have about his risky nuclear plan but all they got was more of the same nasty negativity and politics ... Peter Dutton demands a mature debate but instead launches personal attacks.'
  — Jenny McAllister

'It's more than strange that we have a Coalition proposal for public ownership while Labor is looking to drive private investment.'
  — Tony Wood, Grattan Institute

Peter Broelman, *The Advertiser*

John Shakespeare, *The Sydney Morning Herald*

Panel 1: COALITION ENERGY POLICY PATHWAY

Panel 2: THE ROLLOUT OF DELAYABLES

Panel 4: APART FROM OUR LACK OF COSTINGS, REAL TIMELINES, FEASIBLE DESIGNS, WASTE STORAGE SITES ... OH ... AND UNATTAINABLE FEDERAL AND STATE LEGISLATION CHANGES ... DOES ANYONE HAVE ANY QUESTIONS?

Matt Golding, *The Age*

Glen Le Lievre, *Patreon*

meanwhile, on the narrow path

David Rowe, *Australian Financial Review*

'I think we've always felt that it was a bit too soon to declare victory.'
— Michele Bullock, RBA governor

'This is not the time for scorched-earth austerity. It would not be wise when people are doing it tough and when the economy is soft for us to slash and burn in this budget.'
— Jim Chalmers

Harry Bruce, *Cairns Post*

Fiona Katauskas, *The Guardian*

Matt Golding, *The Age*

'This was … legislation put in place five years ago. Prior to the pandemic, prior to the two wars, prior to that long tail that occurred with the pandemic. You remember at the time, the then Reserve Bank governor was saying that interest rates would stay at 0.1 per cent. Now there have been 13 increases. And what you can't do if you know that you are going in the wrong direction is just stubbornly stay on the same road. So it was a very big call, but it was absolutely the right call.'
— Anthony Albanese

'The most egregious breach of trust and promise by a prime minister in recent history.'
— Peter Dutton

'Their policy is to go to the election to jack up taxes on middle Australia in order to pay for an even bigger tax cut for people on high incomes, Sussan Ley has made that clear.'
— Jim Chalmers

Andrew Dyson, *The Age*

David Pope, *The Canberra Times*

They roared their terrible roars and gnashed their terrible teeth and rolled their terrible eyes as they watched their tax cut sail off into the night.

Glen Le Lievre, *Patreon*

'Labor lied about these tax cuts and now they have lied about what I've said. Our position is that the stage-three tax cuts should be implemented as designed and endorsed by the Australian people at the last election.'
— Sussan Ley

'Our opponents have had a few positions. Not sure what theirs is today. First they said they were against it. They hadn't seen it but they were against it. Then they said they would reverse it. They'd roll it back. What that would mean, of course, is additional tax for some 12 million Australians.'
— Anthony Albanese

'We are supporting this change not to support the prime minister's lie but to support those families who need help now … Because Labor has made decisions that have made it much harder for those families and that is the position we have adopted as a party room.'
— Peter Dutton

Alan Moir, *The Sydney Morning Herald*

John Farmer, *The Mercury*

Peter Broelman, *The Echidna*

Matt Bissett-Johnson, *Melbourne Observer*

Harry Bruce, *Townsville Bulletin*

Mark David, *independentaustralia.net*

David Pope, *The Canberra Times*

'Unemployment has to jump 40, 50 per cent in the economy. We need to see pain in the economy. We need to remind people that they work for the employer, not the other way around. There's been a systematic change where employees feel the employer is extremely lucky to have them, as opposed to the other way around. It's a dynamic that has to change, we've got to kill that attitude, and that has to come through hurting the economy, which is what the whole global — the world — is trying to do … to increase unemployment to get back to some sort of normality.'
— Tim Gurner

'These are comments you'd associate with a cartoon supervillain, not the CEO of a company in 2023. Mr Gurner should spend more time running his company, instead of using a public forum to regurgitate his dastardly economic theories.'
— Jerome Laxale

'Reminder that major CEOs have skyrocketed their own pay so much that the ratio of CEO-to-worker pay is now at some of the highest levels ever recorded.'
— Alexandria Ocasio-Cortez

Fiona Katauskas, *The Guardian*

Fiona Katauskas, *The Guardian*

As the cost of living crisis hits harder and harder — it's been a few years now — here are some cost of living hacks you can use every day.

Firstly there is help from the government who have come out to say ...

We had a great big government inquiry and it turns out it is cheaper to shop at a different shop if that shop is cheaper than the one you shop at.

Actually happened

But that's not all! The government is helping you by giving $300 to power companies on your behalf to subsidise your power bill!

Our power bill just went up $300

Can't afford health insurance? Medicare too expensive? Why not avoid getting sick! As an added bonus you will feel great.

A goed? Be? Ob gorz dot. Wod bages you dig I ab a goed?

Have children and then wait for them to grow up and become influencers.

Work harder Flatula, you're older than Caucus and he already has 1,000,000 followers.

Mum!

Do a budget – perhaps you have unnecessary hidden expenses?
- Food
- Health care
- Rent
- Heating
- Spotify, Netflix, Disney plus, Amazon, Noodle, Slump, Ponkybilp, Frotto, Qlomfq, Flah, Blort, Winkledinkle, Kayo, Unclepooper, Snit

I can't live without Qlomfq!

Send your pets out to work!

Yes I know you're the one who spends all day pulling your little cart at the uranium mine Trixie-tinkle, but you still have to give me your wages. Pay the rent cat!

Start a defence contracting company and wait...

Hello! Sorry didn't see you there here is $9 billion.

Late capitalism will kill us all but it also means you can get a heated blanket for $10 from the Scrimporium and stay toasty all winter

NOT MOVING UNTIL SPRING

Requires electricity and staying near power socket

Having principles costs time and money especially if you're running any sort of government best to ditch them before things get complicated.

Better get rid of that spine while we are at it

I've never even used it!

Tell us your cost of living hacks in the comments and I might put them in a cartoon which will save everyone (me) time AND money.

**First Dog
on the Moon,**
The Guardian

Judy Horacek, *The Australia Institute*

'[Labor needs] to read the writing on the wall, understand that people are hurting at the supermarket checkout, and Labor needs to shift its position, join the growing chorus led by the Greens.'
— Adam Bandt

'What we want to do is make sure we go well beyond what this government has done in terms of facing up to the threat of supermarkets to consumers and farmers. They've been too weak to take them on.'
— David Littleproud

'He's now saying that the tail, instead of being at the back of the Liberal Party dog, will be there wagging away in conjunction with the Greens.'
— Anthony Albanese

Matt Golding, *The Age*

Johannes Leak, *The Australian*

David Rowe, *Australian Financial Review*

'We know that internationally there are examples of divestiture, which means that where there's an abuse of market share or that power, then there's a consequence to pay for that — and we have taken a decision as a Coalition to support a regime that allows for divestiture.'
— Peter Dutton

'Now this is the usual half-baked announcement that's been rushed out to try and cover up for the last half-baked announcement, which was the nuclear reactors that they don't have a cost for.'
— Jim Chalmers

'The government sets this system up for failure, it sets this system up for a duopoly and therefore sets the system up for higher airline prices than Australians should be paying.'
— Rod Sims

Megan Herbert, *The Age*

'The only way we are going to fix this crisis is if Labor finally works with the Greens to phase out the massive tax handouts for property investors, like negative gearing, that are denying millions of renters the chance to buy a home'
— Max Chandler-Mather

'It shouldn't be easier to buy your second or third house than your first, but right now in Australia it is.'
— David Pocock

'The Greens will be in the balance of power on a number of bills in the rest of this parliament … We're going to keep fighting for a cap and freeze on rent … This fight is only just beginning.'
— Adam Bandt

'In the five years from this July, we aim to build 1.2 million of them. Our goal is ambitious — but achievable, if we all work together and if we all do our bit.'
— Jim Chalmers

Matt Golding, *The Age*

John Farmer, *The Mercury*

Glen Le Lievre, *Australian Financial Review*

'I assure Australians that more help is on the way.'
— Jim Chalmers

'Before the budget, the government … said it was not able to adopt every "good idea" in the budget. Making sure people have enough money to eat three times a day is not a "good idea". It is a basic responsibility of government.'
— Cassandra Goldie

'We've seen a government that loves to spend, it's their natural instinct.'
— Angus Taylor

'We're not taking lectures from the same Liberal and National clown show which left us … more debt and much bigger deficits.'
— Jim Chalmers

First Dog
on the Moon,
The Guardian

Mark Knight, *Herald Sun*

'Another surplus is a powerful demonstration of Labor's responsible economic management, which makes room for cost-of-living relief and investments in the future. Despite the substantial progress we've made, spending pressures continue to intensify and there's more work to do.'

— Jim Chalmers

'The emphasis on a surplus is a missed opportunity to invest in measures that would lift those on JobSeeker out of poverty … Budgets are a question of choices, and the government has chosen to bank a surplus over measures to reduce inequality or tackle a fall in real wages.'

— Matt Grudnoff, Australia Institute

'We understand that there are still pressures on the budget, including spending on the NDIS, aged care, hospitals, Medicare, and debt interest. That's why we've put a premium on responsible economic management that strikes the right balance between strengthening the budget and funding our priorities.'

— Katy Gallagher

Jon Kudelka, *The Saturday Paper*

Fiona Katauskas, *The Guardian*

Glen Le Lievre, *Australian Financial Review*

'This government is making the biggest commitment to increasing Defence funding over the forward estimates in decades … National security is a big focus of the Albanese government and it's a big focus of the budget.'
— Richard Marles

'It's a travesty of democracy, transparency, and accountability that we have to trawl through papers of the US Congress to find out how much of our tax dollars are going to fund the US war machine.'
— Marcus Strom, Labor Against War

'Only in Defence could $12 billion be snuck into the budget with no details and no explanation, just that it's being put in the AUKUS submarine bucket … Any honest observer of Defence knows it is a black hole that chews up hundreds of billions of public funds and delivers very little. The funding announcements aren't a celebration, they are an admission of failure.'
— David Shoebridge

Jon Kudelka, *The Saturday Paper*

Matt Bissett-Johnson, *Melbourne Observer*

David Pope, *The Canberra Times*

'We have to think differently about what government can — and must — do to work alongside the private sector to grow the economy, boost productivity, improve competition, and secure our future prosperity … This is not old-fashioned protectionism or isolationism — it is the new competition.'
— Anthony Albanese

'To help make Australia a renewable energy superpower, and an indispensable part of the global net zero economy. To more closely align our national security and economic security interests. To modernise and strengthen our economy, in a world built on cheaper and cleaner energy. To grab the vast industrial and economic opportunities from the world's shift to net zero. And share the benefits of those opportunities with every Australian.'
— Jim Chalmers

'If you look at manufacturing in Australia now, it's not made in Australia because it's going broke. It's going broke under the Labor government because of their energy costs, because of their industrial relations impost, and this government continues to do everything to please the union bosses, but it's making it harder for the workers.'
— Peter Dutton

Johannes Leak, *The Australian*

Dean Alston, *The West Australian*

David Rowe, *Australian Financial Review*

'In my 22 years in parliament, I've seen good and bad budgets. But the budget handed down on Tuesday is one of the most irresponsible I've seen.'
— Peter Dutton

'The usual unhinged, nasty, nuclear negativity in the rant which he tried to pass off as a budget in reply.'
— Jim Chalmers

'The Liberal Party is the party of the worker. The Labor Party has become the party of the inner-city elite and Greens. The Liberals value hard work and entrepreneurialism. We want Australians to keep more of what they work hard for. I spoke with minerals industry leaders today because we support a strong mining and resources sector and the benefits it provides for all Australians.'
— Peter Dutton

Harry Bruce, *Townsville Bulletin*

Andrew Dyson, *The Age*

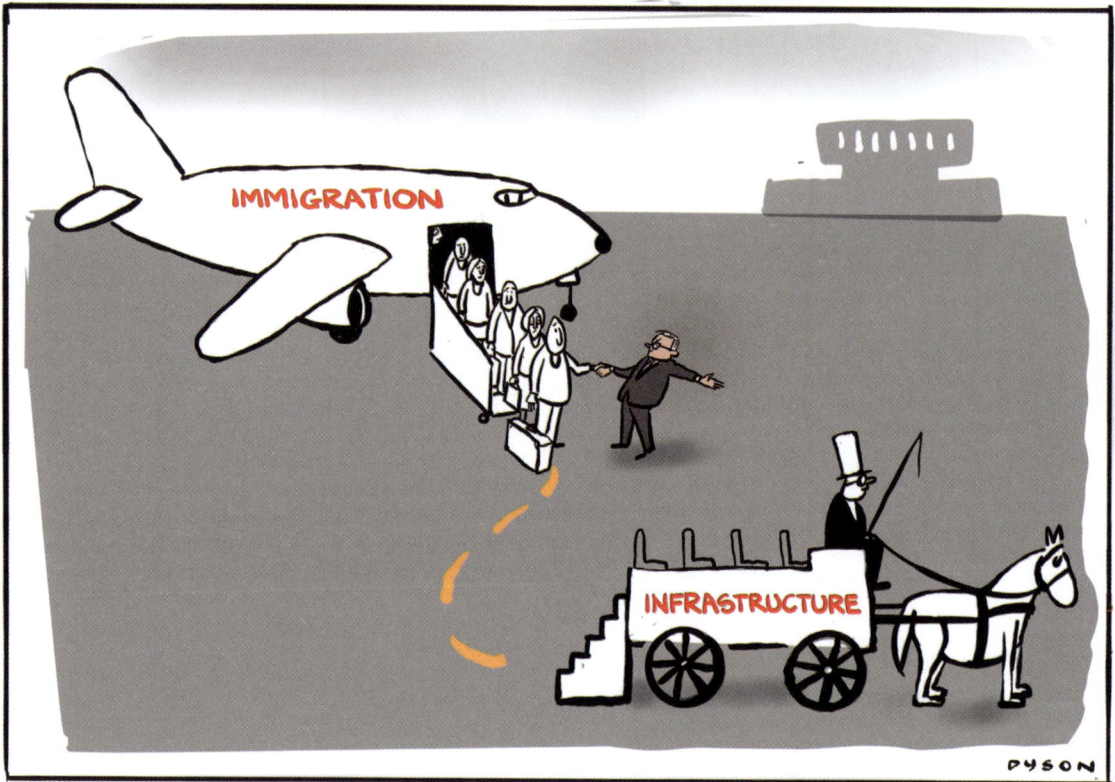

Andrew Dyson, *The Age*

'Australia's migration program is not fit for purpose … successive governments … have responded to challenges through piecemeal reforms which have not addressed fundamental underlying issues.'
— Martin Parkinson review

'We believe that by rebalancing the migration program and taking decisive action on the housing crisis, the Coalition would free up almost 40,000 additional homes in the first year. And well over 100,000 homes in the next five years.'
— Peter Dutton

'Labor has no fiscal guardrails and has abandoned the rules that have supported every budget since Peter Costello.'
— Angus Taylor

'Peter Dutton lowered the bar and Angus Taylor has tripped over it.'
— Jim Chalmers

John Spooner, *The Australian*

Matt Golding, *The Age*

reading the room

Cathy Wilcox, *The Sydney Morning Herald*

'For all employers, the publication of their gender pay gaps is an opportunity to assess their performance on gender equality and take action to improve it.'
— Katy Gallagher

'The gender pay report is now the annual Andrew Tate recruitment drive. It just breeds resentment and division.'
— Matt Canavan

'Mostyn reflects the worst of modern woke Australia … the old boys' club has been replaced with a new girls' club. One new group of oppressors putting the squeeze on a new group of oppressed.'
— Janet Albrechtsen

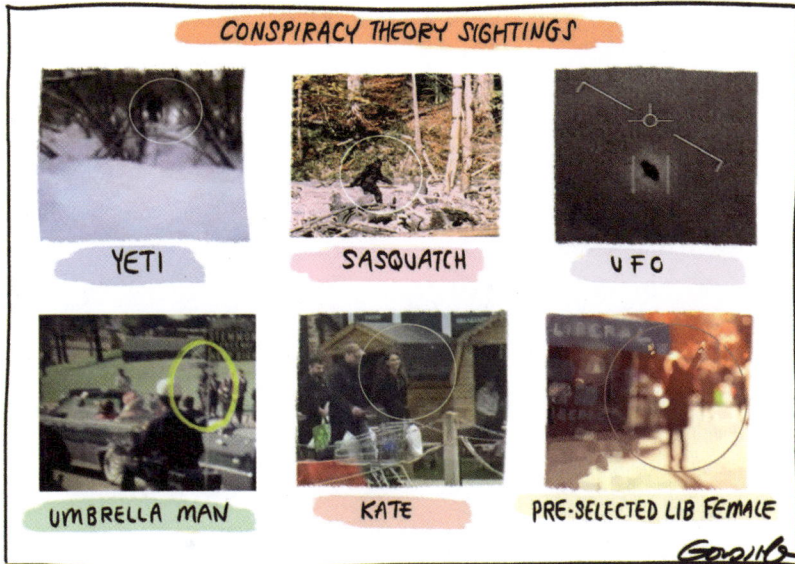

Matt Golding, *The Age*

David Pope, *The Canberra Times*

David Rowe, *Australian Financial Review*

'It is a singular case … Indeed, given its unexpected detours and the collateral damage it has occasioned, it might be more fitting to describe it as an omnishambles.'
— Justice Michael Lee

'Mr Lehrmann raped Ms Higgins … I hasten to stress this is a finding on the balance of probabilities.'
— Justice Michael Lee

'For more than a few, this dispute has become a proxy for broader cultural and political conflicts.'
— Justice Michael Lee

'The cover-up allegation was objectively short on facts, but long on speculation and internal inconsistencies — trying to particularise it during the evidence was like trying to grab a column of smoke.'
— Justice Michael Lee

Johannes Leak, *The Australian*

Dean Alston, *The West Australian*

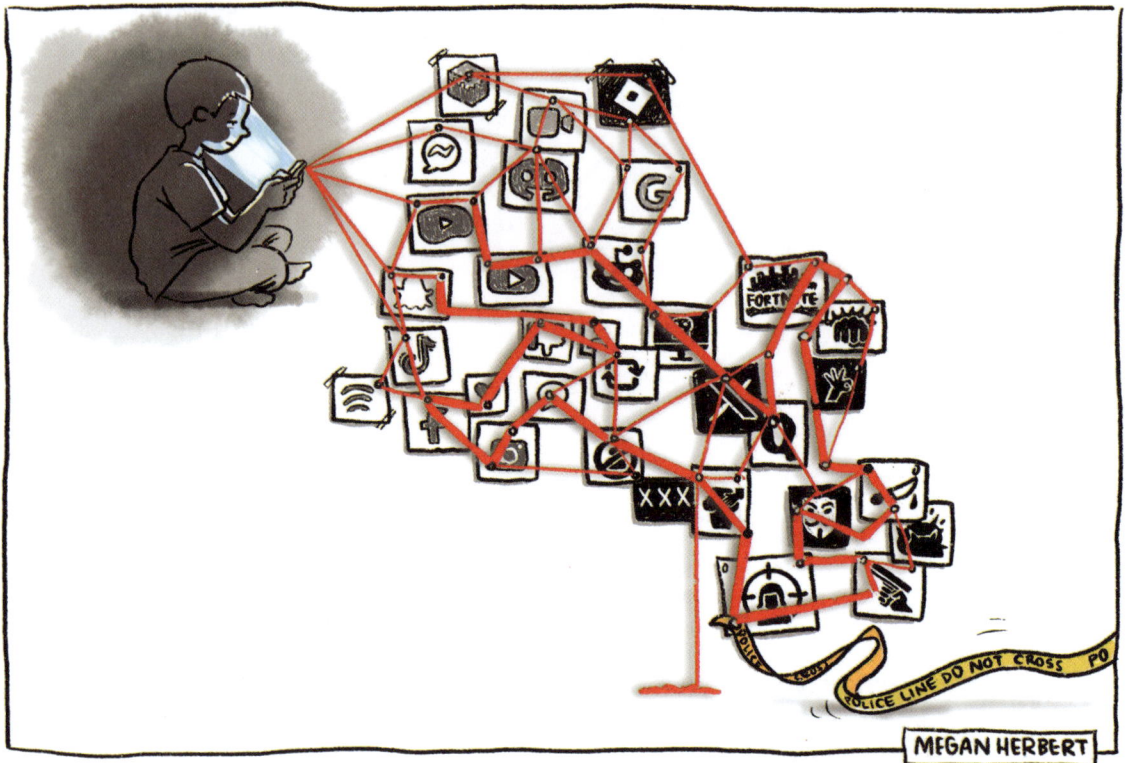

Megan Herbert, *The Age*

'Young women don't feel safe. Older women don't feel safe. That's 50 per cent of the population in this country.'
— Katy Gallagher

'It's predominantly women who are working in these services, who turn up to conferences, who come to meetings, passionately advocating for change. We need those rooms to be as equally full of men.'
— Micaela Cronin, Domestic, Family, and Sexual Violence Commissioner

'Violence against women is a national crisis ... We recognise that governments need to act, but we also recognise that this is an issue for the whole of society. Women should not be responsible for ending violence against women.'
— Anthony Albanese

'I don't know if another royal commission will actually do any good ... Target the funding to communities experiencing high domestic violence [rates instead].'
— Dai Le

Cathy Wilcox, *The Sydney Morning Herald*

Fiona Katauskas, *The Guardian*

Glen Le Lievre, *Patreon*

'Too often we frame this problem as a women's problem, [as if] women need to fix this, but really this is a men's violence problem.'
   — Amanda Rishworth

'It's obvious to me, it's obvious to detectives that … the offender focused on women and avoided the men.'
   — Karen Webb, NSW Police Commissioner

'Implying that the Bondi Junction attacker's mental health diagnosis alone can explain why he decided to attack and murder multiple people is simplistic, offensive, and damaging.'
   — Elfy Scott

'To you, he's a monster, but to me, he was a very sick boy.'
   — father of the accused

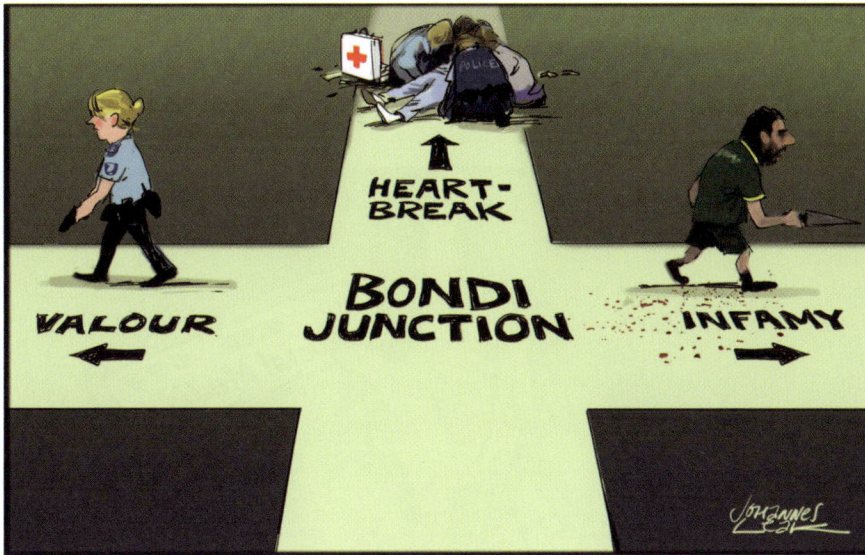

Johannes Leak, *The Australian*

Jon Kudelka, *The Saturday Paper*

down the rabbit hole

Mark Knight, *Herald Sun*

'Many of these digital platforms are now the only way people consume their news, and they need to be regulated and held to account for their behaviour.'
— Sarah Hanson-Young

'I don't think parents are prepared for what deepfake abuse may wreak on their children.'
— Julie Inman Grant, eSafety Commissioner

'The government's reforms will make clear that those who share sexually explicit material without consent, using technology like artificial intelligence, will be subject to serious criminal penalties.'
— Mark Dreyfus

Andrew Weldon, *The Big Issue*

Andrew Weldon, *The Big Issue*

David Pope, *The Canberra Times*

'Australians will shake their head when they think that this billionaire is prepared to go to court, fighting for the right to sow division and to show violent videos.'
— Anthony Albanese

'If you operate in Australia, you should comply with the law. It's as simple as that.'
— Michelle Rowland

'The Australian censorship commissar is demanding *global* content bans!'
— Elon Musk

'Elon Musk should put his big boy pants on and do the right thing — but he won't because he has no social conscience.'
— Jacqui Lambie

'She is an enemy of the people of Australia.'
— Elon Musk

Jon Kudelka, *The Saturday Paper*

Mark David, *independentaustralia.net*

David Pope,
The Canberra Times

Matt Golding,
The Age

Mark Knight, *Herald Sun*

'At X Corp, one of the first steps Elon Musk took was to basically excise 80 per cent of the test and safety engineers, more than half of the content moderators and 80 per cent of their public policy staff, while at the same time letting 62,000 formerly permanently banned users on the platform … If you remove all the digital first responders, the law enforcement, and you open up the jail and let people through, what do you expect you're going to get?'
— Julie Inman Grant

'Tech sucked up our personal experiences and data, organised it with artificial intelligence, manipulated us with it, and created behavior at a scale that brought out the worst in humanity.'
— Maria Ressa

'What we do need to see is much more recognition and onus on tech providers, the tech developers, and also the social media platforms and websites.'
— Asher Flynn, criminologist

Cathy Wilcox, *The Sydney Morning Herald*

'Just as commonwealth law already prohibits discrimination on the basis of race, gender, sexuality, disability, and age, no one should be discriminated against because of their faith. Equally, no students or member of staff should be discriminated against because of who they are. At the same time, religious schools must continue to be able to build and maintain communities of faith.'
— Mark Dreyfus

'It's disappointing that they overlook the concerns of religious leaders and the high regard parents hold for the ethos and nature of their schools.'
— Jacinta Collins, National Catholic Education Commission

'Labor committed to these reforms before coming to power, but discrimination against LGBTQ+ students and staff is happening in religious schools across the country because of gaps in Australian laws that makes it lawful.'
— Ghassan Kassisieh, Equality Australia

Fiona Katauskas, *The Guardian*

Cathy Wilcox, *The Sydney Morning Herald*

the wheels of justice

Cathy Wilcox, *The Sydney Morning Herald*

'The Albanese government has now gotten its pound of flesh from David McBride … I again call on the attorney general to intervene and end this prosecution.'
— David Shoebridge

'He does have the legal power, but he feels he doesn't have the license to intervene in the legal affairs within a government department … I think that's bullshit. That's spelled b-u-l-l-s-h-i-t … These are extraordinary circumstances — it is not in the public interest to continue the prosecution; it would be in the public interest to stop it.'
— Andrew Wilkie

David Pope, *The Canberra Times*

Jon Kudelka, *The Saturday Paper*

Matt Golding, *The Age*

'I believe the First Amendment and the Espionage Act are in contradiction with each other, but I accept that it would be difficult to win such a case given all these circumstances.'
— Julian Assange

'If Julian pleaded guilty in federal court in Saipan, it's because he was pleading guilty to committing journalism. This case criminalises journalism — journalistic activity, standard journalistic activity of news gathering, and publishing. And so this is the reality of this prosecution. It's the case that should never have been brought.'
— Stella Assange

'We wanted him brought home. Tonight that has happened. This is a culmination of careful, patient, and determined advocacy.'
— Anthony Albanese

David Pope, *The Canberra Times*

David Pope, *The Canberra Times*

David Rowe, *Australian Financial Review*

'Several individuals should be grateful the espionage and foreign interference laws are not retrospective … This politician sold out their country, party, and former colleagues to advance the interests of the foreign regime.'
— Mike Burgess, ASIO

'It is inconceivable that you would have a former politician representing their community, representing the country, who then goes and engages with a foreign adversary, and somehow they're allowed to walk off into the sunset.'
— Joe Hockey

'The kabuki show runs thus: Burgess drops the claim, then … the *Herald* and *The Age* miraculously appear to solve the mystery. The villain, as it turns out, is China after all. The anti-China/Australian strategic policy establishment was feeling some slippage in its mindless pro-American stance and decided some new China rattling was overdue.'
— Paul Keating

David Pope, *The Canberra Times*

Peter Broelman, *The Echidna*

Jon Kudelka, *The Saturday Paper*

Andrew Dyson, *The Age*

First Dog on the Moon, *The Guardian*

Christopher Downes, *The Mercury*

Fiona Katauskas, *The Guardian*

Fiona Katauskas, *The Guardian*

'People should be afraid if they've been engaged in corrupt activities.'
— Mark Dreyfus

'We understand that our decision not to pursue the referrals from the Robodebt royal commission will be difficult for victims, their families, and friends. We encourage anyone experiencing distress to seek support.'
— National Anti-Corruption Commission (NACC)

'This is the first public "decision" of the new authority. It screams abdication … a corruption commission that is so stripped of its essential purpose that it really just seems to be a mail room for public grievances.'
— Rick Morton

'It is weak as piss. Hearing this news makes it is clear there is no pathway to justice for the victims of Robodebt.'
— Michael Griffin, Robodebt victim

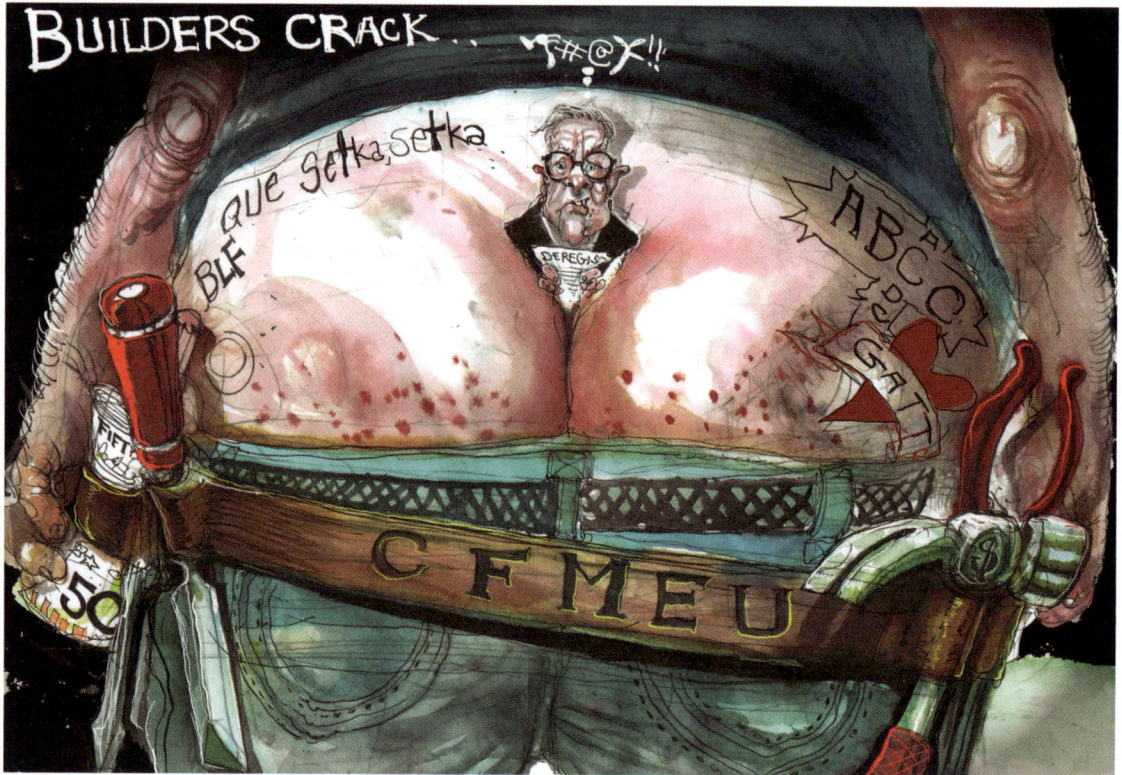

David Rowe, *Australian Financial Review*

'For everyone who's doing the standover, what business person is also engaged? Because for everyone who takes a bribe, there's also someone giving a bribe.'
— Bill Shorten

'John Setka hates our guts, hates my guts, hates Michelle O'Neil's guts, the ACTU as well.'
— Sally McManus

'We will tear this rotten culture out by its roots.'
— Jacinta Allan, Victorian premier

'The way the factional system works in Victoria, you're not going to take to your biggest sponsor with a big stick, are you?'
— former CFMEU official

David Pope, *The Canberra Times*

Mark Knight, *Herald Sun*

the cycle of violence

David Pope, *The Canberra Times*

'Should we be unable to find a way to honest cooperation and honest pacts with the Arabs, then we have learned absolutely nothing during our 2,000 years of suffering and deserve all that will come to us.'
— Albert Einstein, 1929

'Hamas rejects any alternative to the full and complete liberation of Palestine, from the river to the sea.'
— Hamas, 2017 constitution

'Between the sea and the Jordan there will only be Israeli sovereignty.'
— Likud charter

Glen Le Lievre, *Eureka Street*

Andrew Dyson, *The Age*

David Rowe, *Australian Financial Review*

'We have the Israelis right where we want them.'
— Yahya Sinwar, Hamas

'We succeeded in putting the Palestinian issue back on the table … and without a doubt, it was known that the reaction to this great act would be big. We had to tell people that the Palestinian cause would not die.'
— Khalil al-Hayya, Hamas

'Dad, I'm talking to you from a Jewish woman's phone. I killed her and her husband. I killed 10 with my own hands.'
— Hamas terrorist, 17 October

'The enemy will understand that the time of their rampaging without accountability has ended.'
— Mohammed Deif, Hamas

John Spooner, *The Australian*

John Spooner, *The Australian*

Glen Le Lievre, *Patreon*

'We are imposing a complete siege on Gaza. No electricity, no food, no water, no fuel. Everything is closed. We are fighting human animals, and we will act accordingly.'
— Yoav Gallant, Israeli minister of defense

'It is not true, this rhetoric about civilians not being aware, not involved. It's absolutely not true. They could have risen up. They could have fought against that evil regime which took over Gaza in a coup d'état.'
— Isaac Herzog, president of Israel

'Let every terrorist plotting to harm us know that raising a hand against the citizens of Israel will be met with death, destruction, and the deepening of our eternal grip on the entire Land of Israel.'
— Bezalel Smotrich, Israeli cabinet minister

..TAKING STEPS TO PROTECT INNOCENT CIVILIANS..

Geoff Pryor, *Pearls & Irritations*

...WHAT SAFETY VALVE?..

...THE *BIBI* PATENTED PALESTINE PRESSURE-COOKER...

Geoff Pryor, *Pearls & Irritations*

Matt Golding, *The Age*

'We will establish sovereignty in Judea and Samaria, first on the ground and then through legislation. I intend to legalise the young settlements … my life's mission is to thwart the establishment of a Palestinian state.'
— Bezalel Smotrich, Israeli cabinet minister

'We are now rolling out the Gaza Nakba … Gaza Nakba 2023. That's how it'll end.'
— Avi Dichter, Israeli cabinet minister

'The entire Gaza Strip should be emptied and levelled flat, just like in Auschwitz.'
— David Azoulai, Metula Council

'There should be two goals for this victory: one, there is no more Muslim land in the land of Israel … after we make it the land of Israel, Gaza should be left as a monument, like Sodom.'
— Amit Halevi, Likud

Megan Herbert, *The Age*

Fiona Katauskas, *The Guardian*

Jon Kudelka, *The Saturday Paper*

'In the humanitarian corridor from the northern Gaza Strip to the south, what's known as the "drain", there was a line of thousands … They came on donkeys and carts … It felt like the Middle Ages. Destruction all around … They were all holding a white flag in one hand and pressing an ID card against their forehead with the other … Until that moment I also wanted revenge. Now I'm looking at barefoot little girls running on glass that we had broken … and the only difference between them and girls in Ramat Gan is that these were born here and those were born there.'
    — IDF soldier

'There are no innocents in Gaza.'
    — Avigdor Lieberman

'I choose to refuse because there are no winners in war … All people, from the Jordan River to the sea, are suffering from this war, and only peace, a political solution, and the presentation of an alternative can lead to real security.'
    — Sofia Orr, 18-year-old conscientious objector

'I am personally proud of the ruins of Gaza, and that every baby, even 80 years from now, will tell their grandchildren what the Jews did.'
    — May Golan, Israeli cabinet minister

The death of Hind Rajab

Panel 1:
Hind was fleeing Gaza City with her family when their car appeared to come under fire from an Israeli tank. There is a recording of Hind's 15 year old cousin Layan speaking on the phone to a dispatcher at the Palestinian Red Crescent

They are shooting at us.
The tank is next to us

MERKAVA

Then there is gunfire and screams and the line cuts out

Panel 2:
Hind was now trapped in the car with the dead bodies of her family. She was 6 years old. Hind stayed on the line with the ambulance service for three hours.

I'm so scared, please come, Come take me. You will come and take me?

For three hours

TAR 21
TAVOR

Panel 3:
The Palestinian Red Crescent negotiated with the Israeli army for safe passage so an ambulance crew could go and save Hind.

Agreement was reached and an ambulance crew was dispatched

They were never heard from again.

Hind was never heard from again.

KIA PICANTO

Panel 4:
I'm so scared, please come, come take me. You will come and take me?

First Dog on the Moon, *The Guardian*

Glen Le Lievre, *Australian Financial Review*

David Rowe, *Australian Financial Review*

'The only thing that Iran and Israel have in common is that neither of them believes in a two-state solution.'
— Hossein Amir Abdollahian, Iran's foreign minister

'We kiss the hands of those who planned the attack on the Zionist regime.'
— Ayatollah Ali Khamenei

'At my direction, to support the defense of Israel, the US military moved aircraft and ballistic missile defense destroyers to the region over the course of the past week.'
— Joe Biden

'Should the Israeli regime make another mistake, Iran's response will be considerably more severe. It is a conflict between Iran and the rogue Israeli regime, from which the US MUST STAY AWAY!'
— Iranian mission, UN

David Pope, *The Canberra Times*

Cathy Wilcox, *The Sydney Morning Herald*

Matt Golding, *The Age*

'The idea that Israel is now accused of committing genocide is very hard for me personally, as a genocide survivor deeply aware of Israel's commitment to the rule of law as a Jewish and democratic state.'
 — Aharon Barak, Israeli judge, International Criminal Court

'With what audacity do you dare compare the monsters of Hamas to the IDF, the most moral army in the world?'
 — Benjamin Netanyahu

'Hamas strongly denounces the attempts of the prosecutor of the International Criminal Court to equate the victim with the executioner by issuing arrest warrants against a number of Palestinian resistance leaders.'
 — Hamas statement

'Why are there so many arrests? Can't you kill some? Do you want to tell me they all surrender? What are we to do with so many arrested? It's dangerous for the soldiers.'
 — Itamar Ben-Gvir

Cathy Wilcox, *The Sydney Morning Herald*

John Spooner, *The Australian*

David Rowe, *Australian Financial Review*

'It's a precarious moment internationally and if we don't hold onto the law, we have nothing to cling onto … Those profound words "never again" are too often becoming ritual incantations … people round the world are not buying it.'
— Karim Khan, International Criminal Court

'[Judge Karim] Khan takes his place among the great antisemites in modern times.'
— Benjamin Netanyahu

'Antisemitic mobs have taken over leading universities … They call for the annihilation of Israel. They attack Jewish students. They attack Jewish faculty. This is reminiscent of what happened in German universities in the 1930s.'
— Benjamin Netanyahu

'Antisemitism is a vile and disgusting form of bigotry … It is not antisemitic to hold you accountable for your actions.'
— Bernie Sanders

Geoff Pryor, *Pearls & Irritations*

Geoff Pryor, *Pearls & Irritations*

David Pope, *The Canberra Times*

'The ICC prosecutor's application for arrest warrants against Israeli leaders is outrageous ... there is no equivalence, none, between Israel and Hamas. We will always stand with Israel against threats to its security.'
— Joe Biden

'The gut-wrenching tragedy that continues to unfold in the Gaza Strip has laid bare the self-serving nature of the much-vaunted rules-based order ... Why has the West been so ... unequivocal in the condemnation of the Russian invasion of Ukraine, while remaining utterly silent on the relentless bloodletting inflicted on ... Gaza?'
— Anwar bin Ibrahim, Malaysian prime minister

'Despite the illegal and inhumane actions ... Biden has thus far offered unconditional support to Israel. That must change ... [He] must now loudly and clearly say no to the policies of Netanyahu's right-wing extremist government.'
— Bernie Sanders

'Israel is being held accountable for the first time, by the highest court, and by an almost unanimous ruling.'
— Hanan Ashrawi

David Rowe, *Australian Financial Review*

Harry Bruce, *Cairns Post*

hey! you kids!

Glen Le Lievre, *Patreon*

'All of us have a responsibility to prevent conflict in the Middle East from being used as a platform for prejudice here at home … there is no place for antisemitism [or] Islamophobia, in our communities, at our universities, or outside electorate offices.'
— Anthony Albanese

'A two-state solution is the only hope to break the endless cycle of violence.'
— Penny Wong

'Our victory is your victory. Our victory is the victory of Israel against antisemitism. It is the victory of Judeo-Christian civilisation against barbarism.'
— Benjamin Netanyahu

Mark Knight, *Herald Sun*

Fiona Katauskas, *The Guardian*

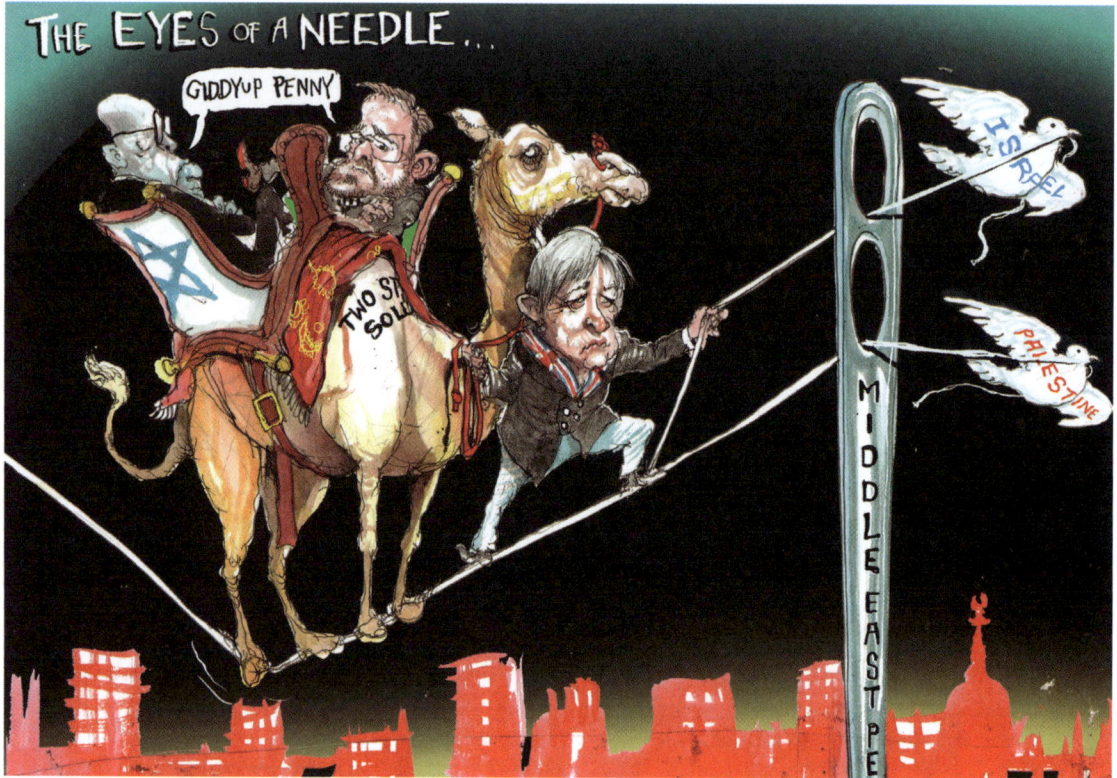

David Rowe, *Australian Financial Review*

'Labor just voted against recognising the State of Palestine … None of us will forget Labor's complicity and cowardice in the face of genocide.'
— Adam Bandt

'The question of recognition [of Palestine] was never before this parliament and yet the Greens chose to message something to Australia and to the world that was inaccurate. And they got headlines around the world that hurt the Palestinian cause but helped the Greens harvest votes.'
— Tony Burke

'The Israel lobby continues to conflate Jews and Israel, including by engaging in lobbying for Israel on behalf of the whole Jewish community. These groups do not represent the opinions of all Jews, many of whom deplore Israel's human rights abuses.'
— Max Kaiser, Jewish Council of Australia

David Pope, *The Canberra Times*

Matt Golding, *The Age*

Alan Moir, *The Sydney Morning Herald*

'I feel very strongly that Palestinians are being collectively punished here for Hamas' barbarism.'
   — Ed Husic

'The House … condemns the prime minister's failure to show the strong leadership required to overcome divisions within his own caucus, to stamp out antisemitism and bring our country together.'
   — Peter Dutton

'The weaponisation or attempt to weaponise antisemitism in this chamber and make it a partisan issue is, frankly, beyond contempt.'
   — Anthony Albanese

'My conscience has been uneasy for far too long, and I must call this out for what it is. This is a genocide, and we need to stop pretending otherwise. I ask our prime minister and our fellow parliamentarians: how many international rights laws must Israel break for us to say enough? How many lives does it take to call this a genocide?'
   — Fatima Payman

David Pope, *The Canberra Times*

Fiona Katauskas, *The Guardian*

First Dog
on the Moon,
The Guardian

THE TIN EAR...

SO, WE'RE DRIVING A YOUNG MUSLIM WOMAN OUT OF THE PARTY OVER PALESTINE ...

...THEN APPOINTING YOU AS A "SPECIAL ENVOY" TO CONFLATE ANY PROTEST AGAINST THE WAR ON GAZA WITH ANTI-SEMITISM...??

OH DEAR, YOU CERTAINLY *SOUND* ANTI-SEMITIC!

David Pope, *The Canberra Times*

'I think it's just a tragic loss of a very capable, principled person … how can the Labor Party speak to these communities if we're not prepared to allow those people that we put into parliament to represent those communities?'
 — Anthony D'Adam, Labor Friends of Palestine

'If you think the Albanese government is bad now, wait for it to be a minority government with the Greens, the green teals, and Muslim independents.'
 — Peter Dutton

'Bigotry at its finest. Fuelling Islamophobia from the very top.'
 — Usman Khawaja

'There's not only been a Muslim candidate from Western Sydney for more than a decade now, there's also two of us who serve as ministers. Maybe try showing some leadership and bring people together rather than tear them apart.'
 — Ed Husic

David Rowe, *Australian Financial Review*

'Trust in institutions is eroding. Provocative, inflammatory behaviours are being normalised … This is really a matter for everyone — community leaders, politicians, the media — watch your words, watch your actions.'
  — Mike Burgess

'I don't think people should be coming in from that war zone at all at the moment. It's not prudent to do so, and I think it puts our national security at risk.'
  — Peter Dutton

'This is what he's done all his life — just attack migrants, whether it's Chinese, Indian, New Zealanders, or now the Palestinians. He's basically Pauline Hanson without the personality.'
  — Jason Clare

Cathy Wilcox, *The Sydney Morning Herald*

Matt Golding,
The Age

so, what's for dinner?

"Piglet, what the fuck?" exclaimed Pooh.

Glen Le Lievre, *Patreon*

'In China we often say when drinking water, we should not forget those who dug the well. The Chinese people will not forget prime minister Whitlam for digging the well for us and now, we are embracing a new 50 years in China–Australia relations. So, your visit this time is highly significant, as it builds on the past and ushers in the future.'
— President Xi Jinping

'We have different political systems, but the engagements that I have had with China, with President Xi Jinping, have been positive, they have been constructive. But we recognise as well we come with different political systems, very different values arising from that, and different histories.'
— Anthony Albanese

'I was asked by Xi Jinping a couple of years ago why I was working so hard with your country. We're a Pacific nation, the United States. We are, and we're going to stay that way.'
— Joe Biden

Glen Le Lievre, *Australian Financial Review*

Glen Le Lievre, *Patreon*

David Rowe, *Australian Financial Review*

'It is the inviolable duty of all Chinese people, including our compatriots in Taiwan, to accomplish the great task of reunifying the motherland. The Taiwan question is the core of the core interests of China, the bedrock of the political foundation of China–US relations, and the first red line that must not be crossed in China–US relations.'
— Mao Ning, Chinese Foreign Ministry

'It is in all of our interests to commit to preventive architecture to reduce the risk of conflict and that communication never be withheld as punishment or offered as a reward. As you know, dialogue enables us to manage our differences; we both know it does not eliminate them. Australia will always be Australia and China will always be China.'
— Penny Wong

'It doesn't take much to encourage Penny Wong, sporting her "deeply concerned" frown, to rattle the China can.'
— Paul Keating

John Spooner, *The Australian*

Andrew Weldon, *The Big Issue*

Cathy Wilcox, *The Sydney Morning Herald*

'We also had a candid exchange of views of some differences and disagreements and agreed to properly manage them in a manner befitting our comprehensive strategic partnership.'
— Li Qiang, Chinese premier

'We will cooperate where we can, we will disagree where we must, and we will engage in our national interest.'
— Penny Wong

'As long as both sides are committed to taking good care of China–Australia cooperative relations, they can transcend the vast distance of the Pacific Ocean and differences … to deliver common progress and win-win outcomes.'
— Li Qiang, Chinese premier

'It was farcical. I ended up feeling like an endangered species — like a panda — being protected by Australian officials.'
— Cheng Lei

Badiucao,
@badiucao

John Spooner,
The Australian

Alan Moir, *The Sydney Morning Herald*

'More than any other part of the world, Southeast Asia is where Australia's destiny lies.'
— Anthony Albanese

'Why must I be tied to one interest? I don't buy into this strong prejudice against China, this China-phobia.'
— Anwar bin Ibrahim, Malaysian prime minister

'Anwar is making it clear, Malaysia for its part, is not buying United States hegemony in East Asia — with states being lobbied to ringfence China on the way through. That difficult task, the maintenance of US strategic hegemony, is being left to supplicants like us.'
— Paul Keating

'NATO barbarians are expanding and gathering at the gates of Asia … Most regional countries want none of it, but four Trojan horses — South Korea, Japan, Australia, and New Zealand — are ready to let them in … Has it crossed Blinken's mind that most of Asia … don't want NATO militarism to infect their parts of the world like the plague?'
— Alex Lo

David Pope, *The Canberra Times*

Glen Le Lievre, *Patreon*

Jon Kudelka, *The Saturday Paper*

'The moment that there is a flag on the first of those Virginia-class submarines in the early 2030s is the moment that that submarine will be under the complete control of the Australian government of the day.'
— Richard Marles

'The AUKUS Agreement is a game changer: it will create a new fleet of nuclear-powered submarines to counter the Chinese Communist Party's threat and influence in the Pacific.'
— Chuck Schumer

'Today's announcement symbolises the huge confidence our close partner Australia has in our world-leading defence industry … Through these collaborations, British industry will grow, and thousands of jobs will be created across the country, delivering security and prosperity to our two nations.'
— Grant Shapps, UK Defence Secretary

'There's no way the UK could afford to build their next generation of nuclear subs without finding some sucker like Australia on the other side of the planet who will chip in billions and billions and billions of dollars.'
— David Shoebridge

Cathy Wilcox, *The Sydney Morning Herald*

David Pope, *The Canberra Times*

David Rowe, *Australian Financial Review*

'This is really a case of us being mugged by reality … there's a lot of AUKUS cheerleaders, and anyone that has any criticism of AUKUS is almost described as being unpatriotic. We've got to be realistic here … They're not only producing about half as many submarines as they believe they need, but they also are not able to maintain the submarines they have.'
— Malcolm Turnbull

'China has focused so strongly and so effectively on building precisely the kinds of forces it needs to prevent the US projecting power … The question for us, is it sensible for Australia to commit itself to go to war with the US against China — a war we have no reason to believe the US can win — in order to acquire submarines that we don't need?'
— Hugh White

'The best parallel … how would Australia imagine that it would undertake, conduct, and retrieve a moon launch?'
— Allan Behm

Geoff Pryor, *Pearls & Irritations*

Cathy Wilcox, *The Sydney Morning Herald*

everyone needs to chill

David Pope, *The Canberra Times*

'He says, "You're not going to be a dictator, are you?" I said, No, no, no, other than day one. We're closing the border and we're drilling, drilling, drilling. After that, I'm not a dictator.'
— Donald Trump

'It's really important to chill, just chill. If President Trump is elected … we're not going over some chasm … this is a perfectly navigable and manageable set of relationships for the next four years.'
— Kevin Rudd

'They're poisoning the blood of our country … All over the world they are pouring into our country.'
— Donald Trump

Mark Knight, *Herald Sun*

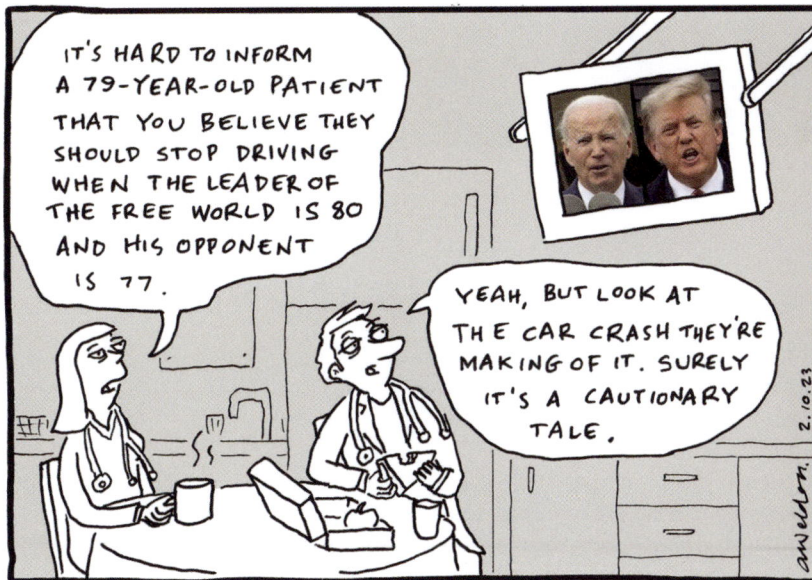

Andrew Weldon, *The Medical Republic*

David Rowe, *Australian Financial Review*

'I didn't have sex with a porn star.'
— Donald Trump

'I'm being indicted for you, and never forget, our enemies want to take away my freedom because I will never let them take away your freedom … They're coming after you and I just happen to be standing in the way.'
— Donald Trump

'Today's decision to grant former presidents criminal immunity reshapes the institution of the presidency. It makes a mockery of the principle, foundational to our constitution and system of government, that no man is above the law.'
— Justice Sonia Sotomayor

'BIG WIN FOR OUR CONSTITUTION AND DEMOCRACY. PROUD TO BE AN AMERICAN!'
— Donald Trump

Alan Moir, *The Sydney Morning Herald*

David Pope, *The Canberra Times*

Glen Le Lievre, *Australian Financial Review*

'I am your warrior. I am your justice. And for those who have been wronged and betrayed, I am your retribution.'
  — Donald Trump

'Don't chase the marginal Karen in a suburb … when we have tens of millions of men that have punched out of the system because of the way immigration and all the society is stacked against them.'
  — Steve Bannon

'Our goal is to assemble an army of aligned, vetted, trained, and prepared conservatives to go to work on Day One to deconstruct the Administrative State.'
  — Project 2025

'Now, if I don't get elected, it's going to be a blood bath for the whole … country.'
  — Donald Trump

Matt Golding, *The Age*

Cathy Wilcox, *The Sydney Morning Herald*

Matt Golding, *The Age*

'The 2024 election is in full swing and yes, age is an issue. I'm a grown man running against a six-year-old.'
— Joe Biden

'Joe Biden had one thing he had to do tonight … and that was reassure America that he was up to the job at his age, and he failed at that tonight.'
— Claire McCaskill

'I really don't know what he said at the end of that sentence. I don't think he knows what he said, either.'
— Donald Trump

'I know I'm not a young man. I don't walk as easily as I used to. I don't talk as smoothly as I used to. I don't debate as well as I used to, but I know what I do know: I know how to tell the truth. I know right from wrong.'
— Joe Biden

Dean Alston, *The West Australian*

Johannes Leak, *The Australian*

David Rowe, *Australian Financial Review*

'Look, I mean, if the Lord Almighty came down and said, "Joe, get out of the race", I'd get out of the race, but the Lord Almighty's not coming down.'
— Joe Biden

'I love Joe Biden. As a senator. As a vice president and as president. I consider him a friend, and I believe in him. Believe in his character. Believe in his morals. In the last four years, he's won many of the battles he's faced. But the one battle he cannot win is the fight against time. None of us can.'
— George Clooney

'I revere this office, but I love my country more … I have decided the best way forward is to pass the torch to a new generation. That is the best way to unite our nation.'
— Joe Biden

Johannes Leak, *The Australian*

David Pope, *The Canberra Times*

Badiucao, *@badiucao*

'This is a time where our country needs a hero, and I believe that Donald Trump is that hero.'
— Trump supporter

'I stand before you in this arena only by the grace of almighty God. Many people say it was a providential moment. It probably was.'
— Donald Trump

'This was an assassination attempt aided and abetted by the radical Left and corporate media incessantly calling Trump a threat to democracy, fascists, or worse.'
— Tim Scott

'We are in the process of the second American Revolution, which will remain bloodless if the left allows it to be.'
— Kevin Roberts, Heritage Foundation

Mark Knight, *Herald Sun*

Peter Broelman, *www.broelman.com.au*

Cathy Wilcox, *The Sydney Morning Herald*

'I go back and forth between thinking Trump is a cynical asshole like Nixon … or that he's America's Hitler.'
— J.D. Vance

'We're done with catering to Wall Street, we're here to fight for the working man.'
— J.D. Vance

'Oh, we'll get this guy who wrote a book, *Hillbilly Elegy,* you know, because all my hillbilly relatives went to Yale and became, you know, venture capitalists."
— Tim Walz

'Project 2025 and others are working on it — to immediately focus on immigration, the forever wars, and on the fiscal and the financial. And simultaneously the deconstruction of the administrative state, and going after the complete, total destruction of the deep state.'
— Steve Bannon

Cathy Wilcox,
The Sydney Morning Herald

Matt Golding,
The Age

PASSING THE RAY-BATONS...

Build·Back·Better

Gaza

BIDEN HARRIS 24

David Pope, *The Canberra Times*

'The idea of selecting the Democratic party's nominee because George Soros and Barack Obama and a couple of elite Democrats got in a smoke-filled room, and decided to throw Joe Biden overboard, that is not how it works.'
— J.D. Vance

'Before I was elected as vice president, I was a courtroom prosecutor … I took on perpetrators of all kinds. Predators who abused women. Fraudsters who ripped off consumers. Cheaters who broke the rules for their own gain. So hear me when I say: I know Donald Trump's type.'
— Kamala Harris

'What has happened in Gaza over the past nine months is devastating … We cannot look away in the face of these tragedies. We cannot allow ourselves to become numb to the suffering, and I will not be silent.'
— Kamala Harris

'Any Jewish person that votes for Kamala, or a Democrat, should immediately have their head examined.'
— Donald Trump

Phil Somerville, *somervillecartoons.com*

Alan Moir, *The Sydney Morning Herald*

David Rowe, *Australian Financial Review*

'We're effectively run in this country, via the Democrats, via our corporate oligarchs, by a bunch of childless cat ladies who are miserable at their own lives and the choices that they've made and so they want to make the rest of the country miserable too.'
— J.D. Vance

'Go ahead and continue to denigrate people … My god, they went after cat people. Good luck with that. Turn on the internet and see what cat people do when you go after 'em.'
— Tim Walz

'The incompetency level is at an all-time high in Washington. The media propped up this president, lied to the American people for three years, and then dumped him for our DEI vice president.'
— Tim Burchett

David Pope, *The Canberra Times*

Matt Golding, *The Age*

David Rowe, *Australian Financial Review*

'These are weird people on the other side … They want to take books away, they want to be in your exam room. That's what it comes down to, and don't get sugarcoating this: these are weird ideas.'
— Tim Walz

'She was Indian all the way, and then all of a sudden she made a turn and … she became a Black person.'
— Donald Trump

'Violent crime was up under Donald Trump. That's not even counting the crimes he committed.'
— Tim Walz

'Some people say, "Oh, why don't you be nice?" But they're not nice to me. They want to put me in prison. They don't want me to be a little bit nasty. They want to put me in prison. Me!'
— Donald Trump

Andrew Dyson, *The Age*

Andrew Dyson, *The Age*

David Rowe, *Australian Financial Review*

'Would [the US] still defend the country if they were invaded by Russia even if they don't pay. No, I would not protect you. In fact, I would encourage them to do whatever the hell they want. You got to pay. You got to pay your bills.'
— Donald Trump

'There will only be peace in Ukraine when we achieve our aims.'
— Vladimir Putin

'Please, do not ask Ukraine when the war will end. Ask yourself: why is Putin still able to continue it?'
— Volodymyr Zelenskyy

'This is a war machine you're facing … They beat Hitler. They beat Napoleon. We got to get this war over with.'
— Donald Trump

Cathy Wilcox, *The Sydney Morning Herald*

Mark Knight, *Herald Sun*

Is it ok to call people names now? Trump has been doing it for years but now the rules have changed. Democrats have begun belittling Republicans with a cruel mocking epithet...

And they don't like it!

Sleepy Joe, Slippery Bob, Disingenuous Digby!

In the US you can call people on the far right fascists and Nazis and for some strange reason it doesn't bother them. Perhaps those insults are overused...?

But whatever you do – don't call Republicans "weird" they get very upset.

Ad hominem!!!

I'm not weird you are!

Is it because Republicans and their ilk want to be seen as representative of "normal" Americans – when what they are is in fact deeply weird and they know it?

More importantly will it win any votes or is it simply irking hard right freaks? Either will do.

You're weird and so is...

your car!

Leave my cybertruck alone!

Name calling has always been part of politics – it can be jolly fun – leftists are called all sorts of mean names – many accurate and some highly defamatory.

You snowflakes are all woke blue haired childless cat lady antifa communists who drink fentanyl flavoured soy milk in the bath!

You say that like it's a bad thing

In Australia calling someone weird isn't an insult – the worst thing you can do in this country is call someone a racist. It's much worse than actually being a racist.

I simply said that all our problems are caused by too many foreigners coming here how is that racist?

There there I'm sure they didn't mean it

In the UK right now people can't decide if the hordes of violent thugs descending on mosques and libraries should be called fascists or merely downtrodden white working class folk.

There is enough for everyone in Britain yet we have nothing, our country has been gutted by the wealthy and society is a collapsing husk. It could only be the fault of...

... people who are even worse off than us.

Get them!

LIBRARY

Who should be called a fascist anyway? Is it the ones setting fire to buildings with children in them or the gleaming nodders in the political and media class who put them up to it?

Good evening and how could this happen in England? Tonight we try to find the people responsible.

TUT TUT TONIGHT

First Dog on the Moon, *The Guardian*

184

Matt Golding, *The Age*

Glen Le Lievre, *Patreon*

Glen Le Lievre, *Patreon*